The New York Times

LOOKING FORWARD

Drone Warfare

THE NEW YORK TIMES EDITORIAL STAFF

Published in 2020 by New York Times Educational Publishing
in association with The Rosen Publishing Group, Inc.
29 East 21st Street, New York, NY 10010

First Edition

The New York Times
Alex Ward: Editorial Director, Book Development
Phyllis Collazo: Photo Rights/Permissions Editor
Heidi Giovine: Administrative Manager

Rosen Publishing
Megan Kellerman: Managing Editor
Greg Tucker: Creative Director
Brian Garvey: Art Director

Cataloging-in-Publication Data
Names: New York Times Company.
Title: Drone warfare / edited by the New York Times editorial staff.
Description: New York : New York Times Educational Publishing,
2020. | Series: Looking forward | Includes glossary and index.
Identifiers: ISBN 9781642822601 (library bound) | ISBN
9781642822595 (pbk.) | ISBN 9781642822618 (ebook)
Subjects: LCSH: Drone aircraft—Juvenile literature. | Air pilots,
Military—United States—Juvenile literature.
Classification: LCC UG1242.D7 D766 2020 | DDC 623.74'69—dc23

Manufactured in the United States of America

On the cover: A U.S. Air Force Predator aircraft lying stationary at
Kandahar Airfield in southern Afghanistan; David Bathgate/Corbis
Historical/Getty Images.

Contents

CHAPTER 3

Doubts and Pushback Raise Questions

CHAPTER 4

International Attention and Relations Intensify

CHAPTER 5

Scrutiny Falls on the Pentagon's Shadow War and Drone Business

CHAPTER 6

Assessing the Effects and Future of Drone Warfare

Introduction

MODERN WARFARE HAS seen revolutionary changes in the 21st century. The foremost development has been that of military drones. These drones include a number of unmanned vehicles, the most prevalent of which are unmanned aerial vehicles, or U.A.V.s. These remotely piloted aircrafts allow the United States military to conduct surveillance on terrorist groups without putting Air Force pilots at risk. They have become so advanced that they can hover for extended periods of time, gathering intelligence on the activity of intended targets while remaining undetected. They have been augmented for combat and have been used in hundreds of airstrikes, killing thousands of people in areas with terrorist activity, including Libya, Pakistan, Somalia and Yemen, among others.

The driving motivation to use drones is the United States' counterterrorism campaign. The war on terror began immediately following the terrorist attacks on Sept. 11, 2001, as the administration of President George W. Bush sanctioned the development and use of this technology to find and eliminate terrorists in the Middle East while keeping military personnel safer in combat areas. Initially, this seemed like it would be an effective strategy, and the budget to develop U.A.V.s such as the Predator and Global Hawk models increased.

President Barack Obama's administration greatly expanded the drone program. Mr. Obama was dedicated to the counterterrorism campaign, particularly as military drones seemed to promise as little loss of American life as possible. However, this dedication fostered the development of policies that expanded battlefields and did not fully eradicate terrorist factions. Foreign relations became

A Reaper remotely piloted aircraft at Hancock Field Air National Guard Base, N.Y., July 19, 2012. From bases in the United States, drone pilots see the faces and families of the insurgents they kill in Afghanistan.

tense because these battlefields could be quiet, discreet and within the bounds of sovereign countries with which the United States was not at war. Intelligence about casualties from drone strikes seemed dubious, and critics of the drone program and human rights groups were vocal about the killing of civilians that were theoretically not supposed to happen if drone activity was as patient and precise as it was purported to be. Questions were raised regarding ethical use and the limits of power — if drone operations could be carried to fulfillment in secret, then where were the boundaries of appropriate use? How effective could public pressure to adjust or end drone activity, from voices both in the United States and the countries where drone strikes occur, truly be under these circumstances? Should the president or intelligence agencies such as the C.I.A. be in command of drone strikes, or should that responsibility exclusively belong to the military?

The Trump administration has continued the drone program and has even sought to relax Obama-era limitations. This has included expanding the criteria for potential targets, which was previously limited to high-level terrorist leaders thought to pose a "continuing and imminent threat." The Pentagon has also sought further improvements to the artificial intelligence used to analyze images collected by drones, which would effectively improve drone targeting.

While the war on terror continues, news of a "shadow war" in northern African nations has gained traction. The presence of Islamic State fighters, Al Qaeda and other extremist groups has prompted further drone activity, including the construction of an American drone base in the Sahara. Apart from these expansions, other nations, including Russia, have been developing their own military drone technology, signaling that the United States might not remain the sole giant in this field. As drone warfare reaches the close of its second decade, the benefits, costs and ethics of the program are still widely debated.

CHAPTER 1

The United States Sanctions Drone Warfare

The implementation of drones for surveillance — and, later, precision target attacks — was a hallmark of the United States' counterterrorism campaign following the Sept. 11 terrorist attacks. The United States military saw the potential of drones to find and neutralize terrorist targets in the Middle East with little risk to its own person- nel and civilians, and as technology developed, military leaders assessed the possibility of drones effectively com- municating with each other without human involvement at all. Pilots controlled drones remotely, and with this new technology came the unforeseen consequence of extreme burnout for military personnel.

A Revolution in Warfare

BY JAMES DAO AND ANDREW C. REVKIN | APRIL 16, 2002

FROM HOMER TO HEMINGWAY, Sun Tzu to Churchill, humans have been fascinated by the violence and plotting, the heroism and sacrifice, the epic theater of what Dryden called "the trade of kings" — war.

But the Pentagon, energized by successes in Afghanistan, is mov- ing ever closer to draining the human drama from the battlefield and replacing it with a ballet of machines.

Rapid advances in technology have brought an array of sensors, vehicles and weapons that can be operated by remote control or are totally autonomous. Within a decade, those machines will be able to perform many of the most dangerous, strenuous or boring tasks now assigned to people, military planners say, paving the way for a fundamental change in warfare.

Already, autonomous sentinels on the ground, in the air and in orbit are probing the battlefield with heat detectors, radar, cameras, microphones and other devices. Some can reveal decoys and pierce camouflage, darkness and bad weather.

In years to come, once targets are found, chances are good that they will be destroyed by weapons from pilotless vehicles that can distinguish friends from foes without consulting humans.

The rapid shift away from people — what the Pentagon calls manned units — to automation has several goals.

Many new devices will be much smaller and lighter, making them cheaper, more fuel efficient and easier to move, advocates contend. And because of their unlimited attention spans, machines should do better at tedious, time-consuming tasks that human warriors loathe, like standing guard or monitoring mountain passes.

But most important, many officials say, remote technology can shield and aid the flesh-and-blood soldier.

"We seem as a society, thank God, very averse to taking casualties," said Dr. Gervasio Prado, the president of SenTech, a Massachusetts company refining book-size robotic sentinels that can be sprinkled on battlefields to listen for enemy vehicles.

"We'll continue putting as much effort as possible into keeping the humans in a safe location and do this dirty job remotely," he said.

In the short run, soldiers, pilots and sailors will still be essential components of any battle, military planners say. This will be particularly true in urban settings, where buildings, tunnels and people create confusing obstacles that no machine will be able to skirt for years to come.

But over time, experts largely agree, remote-sensing and piloting technologies will produce the biggest change in warfare in generations.

By 2020 or earlier, if the Pentagon and its many supporters in Congress and the White House have their way, pilotless planes and driverless buggies will direct remote-controlled bombers toward targets; pilotless helicopters will coordinate driverless convoys, and unmanned submarines will clear mines and launch cruise missiles.

"The promise is enormous," said Dr. M. Franklin Rose, an electrical engineer who is leading a study of driverless ground vehicles being done for the Army by the Board on Army Science and Technology of the National Academy of Sciences. "Robotics can do three things for the future army: keep soldiers out of harm's way, do the laborious and boring tasks and keep going long after a soldier is exhausted. And they have no fear, at least in current embodiments."

Some simple devices, like infrared and night-vision scopes, are available to enemies as well. But no country or terrorist group will have the ability any time soon to deploy these systems so widely and deeply in its forces, many military analysts say.

It is a dream long in the making that has been stunningly accelerated by the war in Afghanistan. There, several pilotless surveillance aircraft turned in unexpectedly strong performances, including the Air Force's Predator and its missile-toting cousin from the Central Intelligence Agency. They piped streaming video of Taliban and Qaeda movements to command posts in Saudi Arabia and the Pentagon, where commanders could then call almost immediate air strikes.

As a result, the Pentagon has requested $1.1 billion, an increase of nearly $150 million, in the 2003 budget to accelerate development of the Predator, Global Hawk and other pilotless planes.

"Why send a marine into harm's way when you can send an $8,000 vehicle instead?" said Brig. Gen. Douglas V. O'Dell, commander of the Fourth Marine Expeditionary Brigade, referring to the Marines' new pilotless aircraft, the Dragon Fly.

Today's advances in military technology are the result of an effort to extending forces' ability to see over the foxhole rim, the next ridge or across a national border and to speed the application of deadly force.

In Vietnam, troops dropped battery-powered listening devices, designed to track submarines, into the forest along the Ho Chi Minh Trail and broadcast the sounds of activity below to crews in planes circling above. The Pentagon also used remotely piloted surveillance drones, including ones armed with Maverick missiles, in Vietnam. But crude technology and limited range discouraged further development.

But the 1990's saw leaps in computer and sensor technology that reignited interest in remote-controlled weapons. In Bosnia, the military tried an Army drone called the Hunter; in Kosovo, it first deployed the Predator. By the time American warplanes began attacking Afghanistan, the Air Force had learned out how link the Predator's cameras to video screens on AC-130 gunships, aircraft carriers in the Arabian Sea and the Combined Air Operation Command Center in Saudi Arabia.

A few years ago, listening devices, called unattended ground sensors, weighed 30 pounds and were lugged into enemy territory by troops. Now they weigh three pounds. One model is designed to be dropped from aircraft. The sturdy sensors detect vibrations and sounds. Using a computerized library of the distinctive noises produced by a host of enemy engines, tank treads and the like, they recognize passers-by.

The next step will be to integrate data from the unattended sensors with information flowing from high-flying drones or satellites, said Dr. Prado, whose company builds the listening devices.

By using different sensors to scour the same landscape and comparing the information, it will be easier to unmask decoys or camouflaged weapons, officials say. As recently as the Kosovo bombing campaign, decoys regularly fooled American bombers.

Leading the Pentagon's remote-control warfare effort is the Defense Advanced Research Projects Agency, which operates out of Northern Virginia. The agency is working with Boeing to developed the X-45 unmanned combat air vehicle. The 30-foot-long windowless planes look like flying "W's" and will carry up to 12 250-pound bombs.

In their initial deployments, as early as 2007, they will be used to attack radar and antiaircraft installations.

The Pentagon estimates that pilotless aircraft will cost less than half as much as piloted fighter jets like the F-15 or F-18, largely because they lack humans.

At first, the aircraft will be programmed to ask human controllers for permission to bomb targets. By 2010, the Pentagon envisions that the X-45 will independently attack targets in designated "kill boxes." Then, "If the aircraft sees a target that matches its memory, it hits it and tells the humans about it later," said Col. Michael Leahy of the Air Force, the program director.

The research agency and the Army are also working on the Future Combat System, a network of pilotless and piloted aircraft, transport vehicles and artillery pieces linked by high-speed communications.

The goal is to make the Army lighter and more nimble. Pilotless vehicles are expected to play a central role. Small hovering drones would peek over ridgetops, while unoccupied helicopters would watch troop movements. Closest to deployment is an all-terrain vehicle programmed to follow a soldier, hauling weapons and other gear.

The Pentagon already has the Hornet, essentially a land mine with a 100-yard reach. When it hears an approaching vehicle, it launches a device into the air that uses a heat sensor to direct a potent projectile down at the target.

Miniaturization is a keystone. Another goal is a "microair vehicle" less than nine inches long that can be carried in a backpack and, when launched, will send images from tiny heat sensors and cameras.

There are many technological and strategic hurdles. First, drones like the Predator require humans to do almost all their thinking. Having unoccupied vehicles accomplish the sophisticated maneuvers envisioned by Pentagon planners will require much greater autonomy, and more powerful artificial intelligence.

"Flying a Global Hawk from California to Australia, impressive as that is, is not as hard as driving an unmanned ground vehicle from here to the Capitol," said Dr. E. Allen Adler, director of the tactical technology office at the advanced projects agency, whose office is about five miles from Capitol Hill.

Second, the armed services have not begun adjusting their strategies to incorporate robotic vehicles. That will take years of study and training, experts and commanders say.

"The real challenge is to mix man and machines," said Colonel Leahy, program director for the pilotless fighter. "It will be a loose ballet at first. But eventually, the systems will be linked to each other, sharing information and deciding among them who has the best shot."

Third, Afghanistan did little to educate the Pentagon on how a more capable military rival might adjust to unmanned systems. The Taliban never learned how to shoot down a Predator, but Saddam Hussein's troops may have bagged at least two last year over southern Iraq. A sophisticated foe might disarm, destroy or confuse pilotless aircraft, rendering them useless or even turning them against American forces.

Finally, debate persists over just how much the military should rely on machines. Most military experts still say the human brain remains the most effective weapon.

"The onboard logic of unmanned combat aerial vehicles will not begin to approach the computational capacity of human brains, making them highly vulnerable to attacks by manned aircraft," Loren B. Thompson, chief operating officer for the Lexington Institute, which studies military issues, testified before the Senate last week.

In the end, said Dr. Rose, the electrical engineer assessing ground vehicles, the biggest challenge will be to design the technology so that to the fighter it becomes an invisible, almost subconscious, extension of the eyes, ears or trigger finger. That will take another generation, he said.

"Already, so many of these young soldiers grew up on video games and computers," he said. "They grew up trusting machines."

Eventually, he said, the new weapons and sensors will slide into the ethos of war just like the autopilot, which was once disparaged by aviators as "Iron Mike" but is now a standard part of airplane cockpits.

"But it'll still be 20 or 25 years up the road before we get to the point where you regard 'Iron Mike' as a member of your squad as opposed to a nuisance," Dr. Rose said.

A War of Robots, All Chattering on the Western Front

BY NOAH SHACHTMAN | JULY 11, 2002

SINCE THE UNITED STATES military campaign began in Afghanistan, the unmanned spy plane has gone from a bit player to a starring role in Pentagon planning. Rather than the handful of "autonomous vehicles," or A.V.'s, that snooped on Al Qaeda hideouts, commanders are envisioning wars involving vast robotic fleets on the ground, in the air and on the seas — swarms of drones that will not just find their foes, but fight them, too.

But such forces would need an entirely new kind of network in which to function, a wireless Internet in the sky that would let thousands of drones communicate quickly while zooming around a battle zone at speeds of up to 300 miles an hour. Such a network would have to be able to deal instantaneously with the unpredictable conditions of war and cope with big losses.

Designing this network is a monumental task. Consider how poor much cellphone coverage is in some areas. Now imagine how much worse it would be with no base towers to direct signals, and with hostile forces trying to jam calls and blow up phones.

An association of nearly 300 scientists and engineers spread across 45 project teams and coordinated by the Office of Naval Research is about a year and a half into a five-year, $11 million effort to determine what it will take to build such a system.

The project is called Multimedia Intelligent Network of Unattended Mobile Agents, or Minuteman (not to be confused with the nuclear missiles). While the program is not about to produce anything like the droid army from the Star Wars movies anytime soon, it has already delivered some important theoretical breakthroughs.

The most important is the network's structure, developed by Mario Gerla, a professor of computer science at the University of

California at Los Angeles. The network will deploy the highest-flying of the A.V.'s, a drone called the Global Hawk, as a kind of cellphone tower in the sky, said Lt. Col. Douglas Boone, deputy chief of the Air Force's airborne reconnaissance division.

Soaring above the battlefield at 50,000 feet or higher, the Global Hawks will communicate with headquarters, transmitting data and receiving commands. The commands will be passed along to a team of lower-flying A.V.'s that will relay them in turn to single drones serving as liaisons for squadrons of A.V.'s.

Despite this basic hierarchy, the network is designed so that any robot in any of the three levels can become the one to relay information to its peers.

"Besides serving as routers, the drones also have to do recon-naissance and carry weapons," Dr. Gerla said. "There is no central control — as soon as you do that you are vulnerable." As a graduate student nearly 30 years ago, Dr. Gerla did work for the federal gov-ernment on the Arpanet, the military precursor to the Internet.

This flexible "network of networks" structure not only allows communications to stay up when individual drones go down but also enables the network to reconfigure itself to maximize bandwidth and to meet goals on the battlefield. Robot planes would constantly shift position to communicate with one another.

This continuous reconfiguration is part of an attempt by Allen Mosh-fegh, director of the Minuteman project, to mimic one of the most elegant of systems for transferring information: the human brain. In the brain, groups of neurons quickly form around a particular goal like reaching for a newspaper, then recombine for the next task, like turning the page.

"A.V.'s will reconfigure in much the same way neurons reconfigure when doing goal-oriented tasks," said Jeffrey P. Sutton, director of the National Space Biomedical Research Institute, which is contributing to the Minuteman project.

The drones will shift the way in which they talk. With "multi-in, multi-out" radios, they will sometimes communicate over several frequencies at once and at other times use a single frequency and lower power. With new methods for the dynamic compression of video under the MPEG-4 standard, the A.V.'s will send images ranging from high-resolution color video to black-and-white still photographs.

The goal is to keep communications flowing, no matter what. Current wireless commercial systems simply drop a connection if congestion builds up or quality deteriorates. That is not a good option in wartime.

Military and technical experts say they are impressed with what Dr. Moshfegh's Minuteman team has come up with so far.

"It's an extremely elegant network, and it's feasible," said Ken Dulaney, a vice president for mobile computing with the Gartner Group in San Jose, Calif. "But it's a dream. There are a lot of challenges."

So far, Minuteman's field tests have seemed more like a hobbyists' convention than a military operation, with model helicopters hovering above toy jeeps with laptops taped to their sides.

Dr. Moshfegh and others behind Minuteman are still unsure of how they will make the jump from motley squads to the tens of thousands of drones that they foresee.

A big part of the problem, Dr. Moshfegh said, is that the routers at the heart of the network are not yet intelligent enough to figure out the right path and speed for sending the nearly limitless amounts of data that would be collected by the drones.

But he is optimistic about overcoming such hurdles.

"If we have enough sources for funding, we could resolve all of these issues in six to eight years," he said, adding, "It's not that complex."

Clark Murdock, a senior fellow at the Center for Strategic and International Studies in Washington, said he was not so sure. On whether Minuteman will be available in several decades or within Dr. Moshfegh's time frame, he said, "My guess is the former."

If and when it arrives, Mr. Dulaney of the Gartner Group sees benefits beyond the battlefield.

"This could be one of those situations where the military figures it out for survivability reasons, and then it goes private," he said of the technology. "By turning receivers into transmitters, it could make wireless networks more robust, more resilient than they are now. It could follow the same kind of path as the Internet."

New Incentives for Pilots of Remote Plane

BY THOM SHANKER | OCT. 17, 2002

THE NEW TECHNOLOGY of warfare is presenting an unexpected challenge for the Air Force as it expands a fleet of unmanned reconnaissance planes: How to attract — and satisfy — pilots who would rather strap into a cockpit and punch holes in the sky at Mach speeds than sit in a trailer watching video to guide a remote-controlled plane.

The white-scarf culture of military aviation is resisting this change. But Secretary James G. Roche of the Air Force is trying to ease the transition to the future by ordering a change in regulations so every hour spent guiding an unmanned Predator plane counts as a flight time when calculating pay raises and promotions.

"These are pioneers, and we won't punish them for helping us into a new era," Dr. Roche said. "Every hour flying a Predator counts as a flight hour."

Dr. Roche said he was aware that many pilots had been brought to their Predator teams kicking and screaming.

"If you're a young F-15 pilot and you're sent to a Predator squadron, your first reaction must be, 'Gosh, who did I offend?' " he said.

"I found that for pilots to get their flight pay, they have to make certain 'gates' — to have so many hours flying," he added. "One of the things that was happening was that these kids were being pulled out of their squadrons — they're all successful pilots by the way. We found they weren't getting the hours toward meeting their gates. And so I changed that."

The reluctance of pilots to join Predator squadrons has been no small matter as the military prepares for a possible mission against Iraq. Senior Pentagon officials say the Predator would probably play a critical role in locating Saddam Hussein's chemical or biological weapons — in particular mobile laboratories and launching systems.

Throughout the armed services, fleets of unmanned aerial vehicles are budgeted to expand. Even so, classified war games operated by the Joint Chiefs of Staff reveal continuing shortages in surveillance of the combat zone.

Solving the problem will require not only more unmanned vehicles but more pilots and crews. The Air Force has just under 100 pilots assigned to the Predator program, and that number is set to grow 50 percent over the next two years.

Secretary Roche said the Air Force had considered assigning non-pilots to Predators, by starting from scratch and training a new generation of technician-operators just for the remotely piloted fleet. But the idea was rejected because officials believed that the pilot corps brought maturity, better training, combat calm and, no doubt, a sense of tradition.

"I wanted to have pilots fly the Predator," he said. "If you try to stand up people who are not pilots, it is like an organ transplant, and I'm afraid the body might reject them."

The Predator, which looks like a slow-flying, upside-down spoon, was one of the experimental weapons that aced its tests in the battlefield laboratory of Afghanistan. Launched from neighboring nations, the Predators were flown by pilots sitting in front of television monitors in trailers hundreds of miles away as they spotted targets, designated them for attack and, in a few cases, even launched missiles carried by the planes.

When not deployed toward the field of combat, the Predators are based at Indian Springs Air Force Auxiliary Field, on the desolate desert range that is part of Nellis Air Force Base outside Las Vegas.

One former A-10 pilot who now flies the Predator acknowledged the frustration felt by many when they are first assigned to the squadron but also spoke of the evolving pride in the mission.

"We feel a bit like the guys in the biplanes in World War I," said the pilot, Capt. Joseph Rizzuto, a commander with the 11th Reconnaissance Squadron at Indian Springs. "At first, they just looked at the battlefield. Then they threw grenades over the side. Then they mounted machine guns and now precision weapons. We will change and enhance what we are doing, just the same way."

Captain Rizzuto emphasized that "the Predator is an airplane."

"It just so happens that my cockpit is detached by 400 or 500 miles," he said.

One of the most respected Predator pilots of the Afghan war is an officer who so mastered the aircraft that she was chosen to fly the super-secret C.I.A. missions in which a new, armed Predator tracked Taliban and Qaeda leadership and then launched Hellfire anti-tank missiles.

Pentagon officials said the pilot, whom they would not name for security reasons, was so concerned that a tour with Predators would limit her career as a pilot that the Air Force arranged meetings with senior officials, including Paul D. Wolfowitz, the deputy defense secretary, who personally expressed thanks for her service.

U.S. Would Use Drones to Attack Iraqi Targets

BY ERIC SCHMITT | NOV. 6, 2002

IN A WAR WITH Iraq, the Air Force would use the same missile-firing drones that killed one of Al Qaeda's senior leaders in Yemen to attack Iraqi air defense radars, mobile Scud missile launchers and possibly sensitive targets in Baghdad, military officials said today.

In Afghanistan, the Air Force flew unarmed Predator planes, mostly for reconnaissance missions or to designate targets for piloted bombers. The Central Intelligence Agency used armed Predators extensively there to attack suspected Qaeda leaders and expanded its killer-drone operations beyond Afghanistan for the first time on Sunday, blasting Qaed Salim Sinan al-Harethi and five associates in Yemen.

About a month ago, the Air Force began patrolling the skies over Iraq's southern no-flight zone with remote-controlled Predators armed with two Hellfires, an air-to-ground, laser-guided weapon used effectively by Apache helicopter gunships against Iraqi tanks in the 1991 Persian Gulf war.

The armed Predators have so far fired three or four missiles at Iraqi targets, including radar dishes, Air Force officials said today. The total number of missiles fired by C.I.A. and military drones in Afghanistan and Iraq is classified, but officials put the number at 70 to 80.

"On targets, it's effective," Gen. Richard B. Myers, chairman of the Joint Chiefs of Staff, said last month.

The Predator, an ungainly, propeller-driven craft that flies as slowly as 80 miles per hour and is guided by an operator at a television monitor hundreds of miles away, has proved a formidable weapon in the campaign against terror.

Last November, a Predator operated by the C.I.A. was used to coordinate a strike in which one of Osama bin Laden's closest lieutenants, Muhammad Atef, was killed in Kabul.

With its ability to loiter continuously for 24 hours or more at 15,000 feet above the battlefield, the Predator can send live video to AC-130 gunships or command posts around the world without putting American pilots at risk.

Its radar, infrared sensors and color video camera can track vehicles at night and through clouds. The video is sharp enough to make out people on the ground from more than three miles away.

"The real advantage, of course, that the Predator brings, armed or unarmed, is the fact that it's persistent," General Myers said. "It's over the target area for long periods of time, and it can move between targets."

In any offensive against Iraq, the Air Force would probably use a combination of armed and unarmed Predators flying from Ali al Salem Air Base in Kuwait, military officials said today. The Predators flying over Afghanistan have operated from an air base in Jacobabad, Pakistan.

Armed Predators could play a role in locating Saddam Hussein's mobile biological weapons laboratories or destroying targets in Baghdad that could be too risky for piloted aircraft.

"The capability of using unmanned combat vehicles, particularly with weapons that can be precisely delivered over heavily defended areas, obviously yields some operational advantages," said an Air Force official.

The Air Force has about 50 Predators, but only a handful are equipped to launch the Hellfire missiles that pack a 14-pound, custom-designed charge of blast-fragment explosives. The C.I.A. has a small, undetermined number of armed drones.

Newer versions of the Predator, made by General Atomics Aeronautical Systems Inc. of San Diego, at $4.5 million apiece, are rolling off the production lines at the rate of about two aircraft a month, Air Force officials said today.

The Predators are not without shortcomings. Like any small plane, they cannot fly in stormy weather, and have been prone to icing. The plane also can be vulnerable to enemy antiaircraft fire. At least nine Air Force Predators and one C.I.A. drone have crashed during missions involving Afghanistan or Iraq since the Sept. 11 terrorist attacks.

The Predator's major combat debut came in 1995 over Bosnia, where it provided sharp images of the battlefield in what the military calls "real time." A year before the Sept. 11 attacks, unarmed C.I.A. drones captured on video a tall turban-wearing man in Afghanistan that many intelligence officials believed was Mr. bin Laden. But the Predators were not equipped to fire missiles.

The use of the armed Predator in counterterrorism was years in the making, coming only after settlement of a long-running argument between the military and C.I.A. over who should have ultimate authority for firing its missiles.

That disagreement, officials said, persisted in the months before Sept. 11 and was resolved only after a Predator missed a chance on the first night of the Afghan war to attack a convoy that some said included Mullah Muhammad Omar, the Taliban leader. The understanding reached after that missed opportunity gave the C.I.A., for the first time, the authority to strike beyond a narrow range of counterterrorism targets.

Fatal Strike in Yemen Was Based on Rules Set Out by Bush

BY DAVID JOHNSTON AND DAVID E. SANGER | NOV. 6, 2002

THE LETHAL MISSILE STRIKE that killed a suspected leader of Al Qaeda in Yemen was carried out under broad authority that President Bush has given the C.I.A. over the past year to pursue the terror network well beyond the borders of Afghanistan, senior government officials said today.

The president was not asked to authorize the specific decision to fire the missile that killed the suspected Qaeda leader, Qaed Salim Sinan al-Harethi, the officials said. But Mr. Bush had been advised that the C.I.A was pursuing Mr. Harethi.

Under the rules that Mr. Bush had approved, his personal approval for specific operations was not required. He had delegated operational control over Predator strikes against Al Qaeda to his military and intelligence team. Officials would not identify the officials who did approve the strike.

The decision to approve the missile launch was made by "very senior officials" below the level of the president who had been closely monitoring the surveillance of Mr. Harethi and his associates, the officials said. They were seeking an opportunity to kill Mr. Harethi in a setting that would minimize the chance of unintentional casualties.

The officials said C.I.A. officials wanted to avoid a repeat of their failed effort last year to use a Predator to kill Mullah Muhammad Omar, the Taliban leader. The strike against him was aborted because of the possibility that others in a crowded house might be killed.

The strike was authorized under the same set of classified presidential findings, legal opinions and policy directives, some of which were prepared after last year's attacks, that have set the rules for the administration's campaign to prevent terror. These orders gave the C.I.A. wide powers to pursue Qaeda terrorists anywhere in the world.

But the Predator attack was the first known use of lethal military force outside Afghanistan.

The missile strike represented a tougher phase of the campaign against terror and moved the Bush administration away from the law enforcement-based tactics of arrests and detentions of Qaeda suspects that it had employed outside Afghanistan in the months since the fighting there ended.

Instead, the officials said, the missile strike demonstrated that the United States was prepared to employ deadly force against individual suspects in countries like Yemen, where Al Qaeda is believed to have regrouped in recent months.

At the same time, the State Department's spokesman today reiterated American opposition to "targeted killings" of Palestinian militants by Israeli forces. The spokesman, Richard A. Boucher, rejected comparisons with Israel's practice against Palestinian militants, saying circumstances were not comparable.

Senior Bush administration officials said the attacks reflected the broader definition of the battlefield on which the campaign against Islamic terrorism would be conducted.

Today, Mr. Bush's spokesman, Ari Fleischer, speaking to reporters aboard Air Force One as the president returned to Washington, said the United States was engaged in "a different kind of war with a different kind of battlefield."

He added, "The president has also made clear to the American people that one of the best ways to fight the war on terror is political, diplomatic, military and that sometimes the best defense is a good offense."

Paul D. Wolfowitz, the deputy defense secretary, said in an interview with CNN, "We've just got to keep the pressure on everywhere we are able to, and we've got to deny the sanctuaries everywhere we are able to, and we've got to put pressure on every government that is giving these people support to get out of that business."

The missile strike did not violate the longstanding ban on the assassination of political leaders because none of the men were regarded as leaders under the law, current and former officials said. Government officials have said since Sept. 11 that the assassination ban does not apply to Al Qaeda.

In Yemen, local officials said they are investigating the killings, and Interior Minister Rashad Muhammad al-Alimi gave the cabinet a report about the blast. Members of the cabinet — who have faced criticism over Yemen's image as a haven for Muslim militants — urged Yemenis to cooperate with security forces in tracking down terrorists.

But Yemeni officials were silent on the question of whether their forces were involved in the operation. Yemeni officials have made clear in recent weeks, however, that they were aware that American drones were active in their area.

The possible risks of the Bush administration's more aggressive approach were immediately apparent. Today, the State Department announced that the American Embassy in Yemen would be closed for a security review.

The Yemenis were killed on Sunday when a Hellfire air-to-ground missile launched by a pilotless Predator aircraft struck the car in which six men were riding in the desert outside Sana, the capital, in Marib Province. All the men were killed, including the intended target, Mr. Harethi, a suspect in the bombing of the Navy destroyer Cole in October 2000.

It was unclear how the target was identified, but the Predator's video can identify certain details like the number of people in the car.

Although Mr. Harthi's name was not widely known publicly, intelligence and law enforcement officials had been tracking his movements for months before the attack, one official said.

The official would not describe the evidence linking Mr. Harthi to the Cole attack, but said his involvement was widely accepted within intelligence and law enforcement circles.

Before the Yemen assault, American counterterrorism operations outside Afghanistan had focused in large part on rounding up terrorist suspects, imprisoning them and seeking to obtain information from them about Al Qaeda's methods and targets. F.B.I. agents overseas and foreign military and security services worked in concert in that effort, detaining several thousand suspects since the attacks on the World Trade Center and the Pentagon.

The strike closely resembled deadly Israeli attacks against Palestinian militant leaders that have been regularly condemned by the State Department, but today Mr. Boucher, the department's spokesman, sought to distinguish between the targeted killings by Israelis and the American strike.

"I think we all understand that the situation with regard to Israeli-Palestinian issues and the prospects of peace and the prospects of negotiation, the need to create an atmosphere for progress, a lot of different things come into play there," he said.

Israel's supporters in the United States have complained about the Bush administration's opposition to Israel's "targeted killings," contending that the United States would act similarly under the same circumstances.

Israel has maintained that the killings are a means of pre-emptive self-defense. Palestinian leaders call the killings assassinations.

Mr. Harethi was not on the F.B.I.'s list of the 22-most-wanted terrorist fugitives in the world compiled after the Sept. 11 attacks.

Although investigators wanted to question Mr. Harethi about the Cole bombing, the C.I.A. did not consult law enforcement officials before the Yemeni operation, a senior law enforcement official said. But today law enforcement officials said there were few complaints about the missile strike or the killing of Mr. Harethi.

One senior law enforcement official said: "I'm ecstatic. We're at war, and we've got to use the means at our disposal to protect the country. You've got to use all your tools, and this is a kind of war which requires us to fight on multiple fronts with all the weapons at our disposal."

Drone-pilot Burnout

BY AARON RETICA | DEC. 12, 2008

ON ITS FACE, it seems like the less stressful assignment. Instead of being deployed to Afghanistan or Iraq, some pilots and other crew members of the U.S. military's unmanned Predator drones live at home in suburban Las Vegas and commute to a nearby Air Force base to serve for part of the day. They don't perform takeoffs and landings, which are handled overseas. But the Predator crews at Nellis Air Force Base in Nevada "are at least as fatigued as crews deployed to Iraq," if not more so, according to a series of reports by Air Force Lt. Col. Anthony P. Tvaryanas.

When Tvaryanas and colleagues surveyed crews who "teleoperate" drones in war zones a few years ago, they found an alarming result: crew members had "significantly increased fatigue, emotional exhaustion and burnout" compared with the crew of a craft that does have a pilot on board, the Awacs surveillance plane. In response, the Air Force implemented a new shift system, in which the number of days off in a row was increased. This year, in March, Tvaryanas released a fresh survey but the results were no better. There was "a pervasive problem with chronic fatigue," Tvaryyanas writes, which "can be expected to adversely impact job performance and safety." The survey also showed that Predator crews were suffering through "impaired domestic relationships."

Why is this? Part of the problem lies in what Tvaryanas calls the "sensory isolation" of pilots in Nevada flying drones 7,500 miles away. Although there are cameras mounted on the planes, remote pilots do not receive the kind of cues from their sense of touch and place that pilots who are actually in their planes get automatically. That makes flying drones physically confusing and mentally exhausting. Perhaps this helps explain the results of another study Tvaryanas published with a colleague in May, which examined 95 Predator "mishaps and safety incidents" reported to the Air Force over an eight-year period. Fifty-seven percent of crew-member-related mishaps were, they write, "consistent with situation awareness errors associated with perception of the environment" — meaning that it's hard to grasp your environment when you're not actually in it.

CHAPTER 2

Drone Policy Development Under President Obama

When Barack Obama started his first term as president in 2009, his administration began further development of military drone use. Handling an already yearslong war and developing policy for an evolving military technology proved challenging. Because terrorist groups such as Al Qaeda were hiding in sovereign countries that were not at war with the United States, conducting lethal operations, no matter how precise, was difficult to justify in those airspaces. Questions were also raised about the morality of the United States' use of drones.

Strikes in Pakistan Underscore Obama's Options

BY RICHARD A. OPPEL JR. | JAN. 23, 2009

ISLAMABAD, PAKISTAN — Two missile attacks launched from remotely piloted American aircraft killed at least 15 people in western Pakistan on Friday. The strikes suggested that the use of drones to kill militants within Pakistan's borders would continue under President Obama.

Remotely piloted Predator drones operated by the Central Intelligence Agency have carried out more than 30 missile attacks since last summer against members of Al Qaeda and other terrorism suspects deep in their redoubts on the Pakistani side of the border with Afghanistan.

But some of the attacks have also killed civilians, enraging Pakistanis and making it harder for the country's shaky government to win support for its own military operations against Taliban guerrillas in the country's lawless border region.

American officials in Washington said there were no immediate signs that the strikes on Friday had killed any senior Qaeda leaders. They said the attacks had dispelled for the moment any notion that Mr. Obama would rein in the Predator attacks.

Mr. Obama and his top national security aides are likely in the coming days to review other counterterrorism measures put in place by the Bush administration, American officials said.

These include orders President Bush secretly approved in July that for the first time allowed American Special Operations forces to carry out ground raids in Pakistan without the approval of the Pakistani government.

Friday's missile attacks hit Waziristan, a remote and mountainous region controlled by the Taliban, in the semiautonomous Federally Administered Tribal Areas along the Afghan border.

The first struck a village known as Mir Ali in North Waziristan late in the afternoon. In a statement, Pakistani government officials said the attack destroyed the house of a man identified as Khalil Dawar and killed eight people. The statement said militants had surrounded the area and retrieved the bodies.

A senior Pakistani security official said four of those killed were Arabs. Pakistani intelligence officials often take the presence of foreign fighters as an indication of Qaeda involvement.

In the second attack, missiles struck a house near the village of Wana in South Waziristan, killing seven people, according to local accounts and Pakistani news reports. The reports said three of the dead were children.

American officials believe that the drone strikes have killed a number of suspected militants along the frontier since last year, including a senior Qaeda operative who was killed Jan. 1 and was suspected in the

1998 bombings of the United States Embassies in Kenya and Tanzania and the bombing of the Marriott Hotel in Islamabad four months ago.

But the civilian toll has angered Pakistanis. A senior Pakistani official estimated that the attacks might have killed as many as 100 civilians; it was not possible to verify the estimate.

American and Pakistani officials are known to share some intelligence about militants, but it is unclear whether Pakistani officials have in any way acquiesced to the drone strikes or helped provide intelligence for them while opposing them in public. Openly supporting the attacks would be untenable for a government perceived as being too close to the American government.

ISMAIL KHAN contributed reporting from Peshawar, Pakistan, and ERIC SCHMITT from Washington.

U.S. Unit Secretly in Pakistan Lends Ally Support

BY ERIC SCHMITT AND JANE PERLEZ | FEB. 22, 2009

BARA, PAKISTAN — More than 70 United States military advisers and technical specialists are secretly working in Pakistan to help its armed forces battle Al Qaeda and the Taliban in the country's lawless tribal areas, American military officials said.

The Americans are mostly Army Special Forces soldiers who are training Pakistani Army and paramilitary troops, providing them with intelligence and advising on combat tactics, the officials said. They do not conduct combat operations, the officials added.

They make up a secret task force, overseen by the United States Central Command and Special Operations Command. It started last summer, with the support of Pakistan's government and military, in an effort to root out Qaeda and Taliban operations that threaten American troops in Afghanistan and are increasingly destabilizing Pakistan. It is a much larger and more ambitious effort than either country has acknowledged.

Pakistani officials have vigorously protested American missile strikes in the tribal areas as a violation of sovereignty and have resisted efforts by Washington to put more troops on Pakistani soil. President Asif Ali Zardari, who leads a weak civilian government, is trying to cope with soaring anti-Americanism among Pakistanis and a belief that he is too close to Washington.

Despite the political hazards for Islamabad, the American effort is beginning to pay dividends.

A new Pakistani commando unit within the Frontier Corps paramilitary force has used information from the Central Intelligence Agency and other sources to kill or capture as many as 60 militants in the past seven months, including at least five high-ranking commanders, a senior Pakistani military official said.

In a demonstration Sunday in the Khyber Agency, a tribal district, Pakistani commandos repelled a mock Taliban ambush.

Four weeks ago, the commandos captured a Saudi militant linked to Al Qaeda here in this town in the Khyber Agency, one of the tribal areas that run along the border with Afghanistan.

Yet the main commanders of the Pakistani Taliban, including its leader, Baitullah Mehsud, and its leader in the Swat region, Maulana Fazlullah, remain at large. And senior American military officials remain frustrated that they have been unable to persuade the chief of the Pakistani Army, Gen. Ashfaq Parvez Kayani, to embrace serious counterinsurgency training for the army itself.

General Kayani, who is visiting Washington this week as a White House review on policy for Afghanistan and Pakistan gets under way, will almost certainly be asked how the Pakistani military can do more to eliminate Al Qaeda and the Taliban from the tribal areas.

The American officials acknowledge that at the very moment when Washington most needs Pakistan's help, the greater tensions between

Pakistan and India since the terrorist attacks in Mumbai last November have made the Pakistani Army less willing to shift its attention to the Qaeda and Taliban threat.

Officials from both Pakistan and the United States agreed to disclose some details about the American military advisers and the enhanced intelligence sharing to help dispel impressions that the missile strikes were thwarting broader efforts to combat a common enemy. They spoke on condition of anonymity, citing the increasingly powerful anti-American segment of the Pakistani population.

The Pentagon had previously said about two dozen American trainers conducted training in Pakistan late last year. More than half the members of the new task force are Special Forces advisers; the rest are combat medics, communications experts and other specialists. Both sides are encouraged by the new collaboration between the American and Pakistani military and intelligence agencies against the militants.

"The intelligence sharing has really improved in the past few months," said Talat Masood, a retired army general and a military analyst. "Both sides realize it's in their common interest."

Intelligence from Pakistani informants has been used to bolster the accuracy of missile strikes from remotely piloted Predator and Reaper aircraft against the militants in the tribal areas, officials from both countries say.

More than 30 attacks by the aircraft have been conducted since last August, most of them after President Zardari took office in September. A senior American military official said that 9 of 20 senior Qaeda and Taliban commanders in Pakistan had been killed by those strikes.

In addition, a small team of Pakistani air defense controllers working in the United States Embassy in Islamabad ensures that Pakistani F-16 fighter-bombers conducting missions against militants in the tribal areas do not mistakenly hit remotely piloted American aircraft flying in the same area or a small number of C.I.A. operatives on the ground, a second senior Pakistani officer said.

The newly minted 400-man Pakistani paramilitary commando unit is a good example of the new cooperation. As part of the Frontier Corps, which operates in the tribal areas, the new Pakistani commandos fall under a chain of command separate from the 500,000-member army, which is primarily trained to fight Pakistan's archenemy, India.

The commandos are selected from the overall ranks of the Frontier Corps and receive seven months of intensive training from Pakistani and American Special Forces.

The C.I.A. helped the commandos track the Saudi militant linked to Al Qaeda, Zabi al-Taifi, for more than a week before the Pakistani forces surrounded his safe house in the Khyber Agency. The Pakistanis seized him, along with seven Pakistani and Afghan insurgents, in a dawn raid on Jan. 22, with a remotely piloted C.I.A. plane hovering overhead and personnel from the C.I.A. and Pakistan's main spy service closely monitoring the mission, a senior Pakistani officer involved in the operation said.

Still, there are tensions between the sides. Pakistani F-16's conduct about a half-dozen combat missions a day against militants, but Pakistani officers say they could do more if the Pentagon helped upgrade the jets to fight at night and provided satellite-guided bombs and updated satellite imagery.

General Kayani was expected to take a long shopping list for more transport and combat helicopters to Washington. The question of more F-16's — which many in Congress assert are intended for the Indian front — will also come up, Pakistani officials said.

The United States missile strikes, which have resulted in civilian casualties, have stirred heated debate among senior Pakistani government and military officials, despite the government's private support for the attacks.

One American official described General Kayani, who is known to be sensitive about the necessity of public support for the army, as very concerned that the American strikes had undermined the army's authority.

"These strikes are counterproductive," Owais Ahmed Ghani, the governor of North-West Frontier Province, said in an interview in his office in Peshawar. "This is looking for a quick fix, when all it will do is attract more jihadis."

Pakistani Army officers say the American strikes draw retaliation against Pakistani troops in the tribal areas, whose convoys and bases are bombed or attacked with rockets after each United States missile strike.

ERIC SCHMITT reported from Bara, Peshawar and Islamabad, Pakistan, and **JANE PERLEZ** from Islamabad.

The Moral Case for Drones

BY SCOTT SHANE | JULY 14, 2012

WASHINGTON — For streamlined, unmanned aircraft, drones carry a lot of baggage these days, along with their Hellfire missiles. Some people find the very notion of killer robots deeply disturbing. Their lethal operations inside sovereign countries that are not at war with the United States raise contentious legal questions. They have become a radicalizing force in some Muslim countries. And proliferation will inevitably put them in the hands of odious regimes.

But most critics of the Obama administration's aggressive use of drones for targeted killing have focused on evidence that they are unintentionally killing innocent civilians. From the desolate tribal regions of Pakistan have come heartbreaking tales of families wiped out by mistake and of children as collateral damage in the campaign against Al Qaeda. And there are serious questions about whether American officials have understated civilian deaths.

So it may be a surprise to find that some moral philosophers, political scientists and weapons specialists believe armed, unmanned aircraft offer marked moral advantages over almost any other tool of warfare.

"I had ethical doubts and concerns when I started looking into this," said Bradley J. Strawser, a former Air Force officer and an assistant professor of philosophy at the Naval Postgraduate School. But after a concentrated study of remotely piloted vehicles, he said, he concluded that using them to go after terrorists not only was ethically permissible but also might be ethically obligatory, because of their advantages in identifying targets and striking with precision.

"You have to start by asking, as for any military action, is the cause just?" Mr. Strawser said. But for extremists who are indeed plotting violence against innocents, he said, "all the evidence we have so far suggests that drones do better at both identifying the terrorist and avoiding collateral damage than anything else we have."

Since drone operators can view a target for hours or days in advance of a strike, they can identify terrorists more accurately than ground troops or conventional pilots. They are able to time a strike when innocents are not nearby and can even divert a missile after firing if, say, a child wanders into range.

Clearly, those advantages have not always been used competently or humanely; like any other weapon, armed drones can be used recklessly or on the basis of flawed intelligence. If an operator targets the wrong house, innocents will die.

Moreover, any analysis of actual results from the Central Intelligence Agency's strikes in Pakistan, which has become the world's unwilling test ground for the new weapon, is hampered by secrecy and wildly varying casualty reports. But one rough comparison has found that even if the highest estimates of collateral deaths are accurate, the drones kill fewer civilians than other modes of warfare.

Avery Plaw, a political scientist at the University of Massachusetts, put the C.I.A. drone record in Pakistan up against the ratio of combatant deaths to civilian deaths in other settings. Mr. Plaw considered four studies of drone deaths in Pakistan that estimated the proportion of civilian victims at 4 percent, 6 percent, 17 percent and 20 percent respectively.

But even the high-end count of 20 percent was considerably lower than the rate in other settings, he found. When the Pakistani Army went after militants in the tribal area on the ground, civilians were 46 percent of those killed. In Israel's targeted killings of militants from Hamas and other groups, using a range of weapons from bombs to missile strikes, the collateral death rate was 41 percent, according to an Israeli human rights group.

In conventional military conflicts over the last two decades, he found that estimates of civilian deaths ranged from about 33 percent to more than 80 percent of all deaths.

Mr. Plaw acknowledged the limitations of such comparisons, which mix different kinds of warfare. But he concluded, "A fair-minded evaluation of the best data we have available suggests that the drone program compares favorably with similar operations and contemporary armed conflict more generally."

By the count of the Bureau of Investigative Journalism in London, which has done perhaps the most detailed and skeptical study of the strikes, the C.I.A. operators are improving their performance. The bureau has documented a notable drop in the civilian proportion of drone casualties, to 16 percent of those killed in 2011 from 28 percent in 2008. This year, by the bureau's count, just three of the 152 people killed in drone strikes through July 7 were civilians.

The drone's promise of precision killing and perfect safety for operators is so seductive, in fact, that some scholars have raised a different moral question: Do drones threaten to lower the threshold for lethal violence?

"In the just-war tradition, there's the notion that you only wage war as a last resort," said Daniel R. Brunstetter, a political scientist at the University of California at Irvine who fears that drones are becoming "a default strategy to be used almost anywhere."

With hundreds of terrorist suspects killed under President Obama and just one taken into custody overseas, some question whether drones have become not a more precise alternative to bombing but a convenient substitute for capture. If so, drones may actually be encouraging unnecessary killing.

Few imagined such debates in 2000, when American security officials first began to think about arming the Predator surveillance drone, with which they had spotted Osama bin Laden at his Afghanistan base, said Henry A. Crumpton, then deputy chief of the C.I.A.'s counterterrorism center, who tells the story in his recent memoir, "The Art of Intelligence."

"We never said, 'Let's build a more humane weapon,' " Mr. Crumpton said. "We said, 'Let's be as precise as possible, because that's our mission — to kill Bin Laden and the people right around him.' "

Since then, Mr. Crumpton said, the drone war has prompted an intense focus on civilian casualties, which in a YouTube world have become harder to hide. He argues that technological change is producing a growing intolerance for the routine slaughter of earlier wars.

"Look at the firebombing of Dresden, and compare what we're doing today," Mr. Crumpton said. "The public's expectations have been raised dramatically around the world, and that's good news."

SCOTT SHANE is a national security reporter for The New York Times.

The Moral Hazard of Drones

OPINION | BY JOHN KAAG AND SARAH KREPS | JULY 22, 2012

AS THE DEBATE on the morality of the United States' use of unmanned aerial vehicles ("U.A.V.'s," also known as drones) has intensified in recent weeks, several news and opinion articles have appeared in the media. Two, in particular, both published this month, reflect the current ethical divide on the issue. A feature article in Esquire by Tom Junod censured the "Lethal Presidency of Barack Obama" for the administration's policy of targeted killings of suspected militants; another, "The Moral Case for Drones," a news analysis by The Times' Scott Shane, gathered opinions from experts that implicitly commended the administration for replacing Dresden-style strategic bombing with highly precise attacks that minimize collateral damage.

Amid this discussion, we suggest that an allegory might be helpful to illustrate some of the many moral perils of drone use that have been overlooked. It shows that our attempts to avoid obvious ethical pitfalls of actions like firebombing may leave us vulnerable to other, more subtle, moral dangers.

While drones have become the weapons of our age, the moral dilemma that drone warfare presents is not new. In fact, it is very, very old:

Once upon a time, in a quiet corner of the Middle East, there lived a shepherd named Gyges. Despite the hardships in his life Gyges was relatively satisfied with his meager existence. Then, one day, he found a ring buried in a nearby cave.

This was no ordinary ring; it rendered its wearer invisible. With this new power, Gyges became increasingly dissatisfied with his simple life. Before long, he seduced the queen of the land and began to plot the overthrow of her husband. One evening, Gyges placed the ring on his finger, sneaked into the royal palace, and murdered the king.

In his "Republic," Plato recounts this tale, but does not tell us the details of the murder. Still, we can rest assured that, like any violent death, it was not a pleasant affair. However, the story ends well, at least for Gyges. He marries the queen and assumes the position of king.

This story, which is as old as Western ethics itself, is meant to elicit a particular moral response from us: disgust. So why do we find Plato's story so appalling? Maybe it's the way that the story replaces moral justification with practical efficiency: Gyges' being able to commit murder without getting caught, without any real difficulty, does not mean he is justified in doing so. (Expediency is not necessarily a virtue.)

Maybe it's the way that Gyges' ring obscures his moral culpability: it's difficult to blame a person you can't see, and even harder to bring them to justice.

Maybe it's that Gyges is successful in his plot: a wicked act not only goes unpunished, but is rewarded.

Maybe it's the nagging sense that any kingdom based on such deception could not be a just one: what else might happen in such a kingdom under the cover of darkness?

Our disgust with Gyges could be traced to any one of these concerns, or to all of them.

One might argue that the myth of Gyges is a suitable allegory to describe the combatants who have attacked and killed American civilians and troops in the last 10 years. A shepherd from the Middle East discovers that he has the power of invisibility, the power to strike a fatal blow against a more powerful adversary, the power to do so without getting caught, the power to benefit from his deception. These, after all, are the tactics of terrorism.

But the myth of Gyges is really a story about modern counterterrorism, not terrorism.

We believe a stronger comparison can be made between the myth and the moral dangers of employing precision guided munitions and drone technologies to target suspected terrorists. What is distinctive about the tale of Gyges is the ease with which he can commit murder and get away scot-free. The technological advantage provided by the ring ends up serving as the justification of its use.

Terrorists, whatever the moral value of their deeds, may be found and punished; as humans they are subject to retribution, whether it be corporal or legal. They may lose or sacrifice their lives. They may, in fact, be killed in the middle of the night by a drone. Because remote controlled machines cannot suffer these consequences, and the humans who operate them do so at a great distance, the myth of Gyges is more a parable of modern counterterrorism than it is about terrorism.

Only recently has the use of drones begun to touch on questions of morality. Perhaps it's because the answers to these questions appear self-evident. What could be wrong with the use of unmanned aerial vehicles? After all, they limit the cost of war, in terms of both blood and treasure. The U.S. troops who operate them can maintain safer stand-off positions in Eastern Europe or at home. And armed with precision-guided munitions, these drones are said to limit collateral damage. In 2009, Leon Panetta, who was then the director of the Central Intelligence Agency, said, U.A.V.'s are "very precise and very limited in terms of collateral damage … the only game in town in terms of confronting or trying to disrupt the al Qaeda leadership." What could be wrong with all this?

Quite a bit, it turns out.

Return, for a minute, to the moral disgust that Gyges evokes in us. Gyges also risked very little in attacking the king. The success of his mission was almost assured, thanks to the technological advantage of his ring. Gyges could sneak past the king's guards unscathed, so he did not need to kill anyone he did not intend on killing. These are the facts of the matter.

What we find unsettling here is the idea that these facts could be confused for moral justification. Philosophers find this confusion particularly abhorrent and guard against it with the only weapon they have: a distinction. The "fact-value distinction" holds that statements of fact should never be confused with statements of value. More strongly put, this distinction means that statements of fact do not even imply statements of value. "Can" does not imply "ought." To say that we can target individuals without incurring troop casualties does not imply that we ought to.

This seems so obvious. But, as Peter W. Singer noted earlier this year in The Times, when the Obama administration was asked why continued U.S. military strikes in the Middle East did not constitute a violation of the 1973 War Powers Resolution, it responded that such activities did not "involve the presence of U.S. ground troops, U.S. casualties or a serious threat thereof." The justification of these strikes rested solely on their ease. The Ring of Gyges has the power to obscure the obvious.

This issue has all the hallmarks of what economists and philosophers call a "moral hazard" — a situation in which greater risks are taken by individuals who are able to avoid shouldering the cost associated with these risks. It thus seems wise, if not convenient, to underscore several ethical points if we are to avoid our own "Gyges moment."

First, we might remember Marx's comment that "the windmill gives you a society with the feudal lord; the steam engine gives you one with the industrial capitalist." And precision guided munitions and drones give you a society with perpetual asymmetric wars.

The creation of technology is a value-laden enterprise. It creates the material conditions of culture and society and therefore its creation should be regarded as always already moral and political in nature. However, technology itself (the physical stuff of robotic warfare) is neither smart nor dumb, moral nor immoral. It can be used more or less precisely, but precision and efficiency are not inherently morally good. Imagine a very skilled dentist who painlessly removes the wrong tooth. Imagine a drone equipped with a precision guided munition that kills a completely innocent person, but spares the people who live in his or her neighborhood. The use of impressive technologies does not grant one impressive moral insight. Indeed, as Gyges demonstrates, the opposite can be the case.

Second, assassination and targeted killings have always been in the repertoires of military planners, but never in the history of warfare have they been so cheap and easy. The relatively low number of troop casualties for a military that has turned to drones means that there is relatively little domestic blowback against these wars. The United States and its allies have created the material conditions whereby these wars can carry on indefinitely. The non-combatant casualty rates in populations that are attacked by drones are slow and steady, but they add up. That the casualty rates are relatively low by historical standards — this is no Dresden — is undoubtedly a good thing, but it may allow the international media to overlook pesky little facts like the slow accretion of foreign casualties.

Third, the impressive expediency and accuracy in drone targeting may also allow policymakers and strategists to become lax in their moral decision-making about who exactly should be targeted. Consider the stark contrast between the ambiguous language used to define legitimate targets and the specific technical means a military uses to neutralize these targets. The terms "terrorist," "enemy combatant," and "contingent threat" are extremely vague and do very little to articulate the legitimacy of military targets. In contrast, the technical capabilities of weapon systems define and "paint" these targets with ever-greater definition. As weaponry becomes more precise, the language of warfare has become more ambiguous.

This ambiguity has, for example, altered the discourse surrounding the issue of collateral damage. There are two very different definitions of collateral damage, and these definitions affect the truth of the following statement: "Drone warfare and precision guided munitions limit collateral damage." One definition views collateral damage as the inadvertent destruction of property and persons in a given attack. In other words, collateral damage refers to "stuff we don't mean to blow up." Another definition characterizes collateral damage as objects or individuals "that would not be lawful military targets in the circumstances ruling at the time." In other words, collateral damage refers to "the good guys." Since 1998, this is the definition that has been used. What is the difference between these definitions?

The first is a description of technical capabilities (being able to hit X while not hitting Y); the second is a normative and indeed legal judgment about who is and is not innocent (and therefore who is a legitimate target and who is not). The first is a matter of fact, the second a matter of value. There is an important difference between these statements, and they should not be confused.

Fourth, questions of combatant status should be the subject of judicial review and moral scrutiny. Instead, if these questions are asked at all, they are answered as if they were mere matters of fact, unilaterally, behind closed doors, rather than through transparent due process. That moral reasoning has become even more slippery of late, as the American government has implied that all military aged males in a strike area are legitimate targets: a "guilt by association" designation.

Finally, as the strategic repertoires of modern militaries expand to include drones and precision guided munitions, it is not at all clear that having more choices leads strategists to make better and more informed ones. In asking, "Is More Choice Better Than Less?" the philosopher Gerald Dworkin once argued that the answer is "not always." In the words of Kierkegaard: "In possibility everything is possible. Hence in possibility one can go astray in all possible ways."

Some might object that these guidelines set unrealistically high expectations on military strategists and policymakers. They would probably be right. But no one — except Gyges — said that being ethical was easy.

JOHN KAAG is an assistant professor of philosophy at the University of Massachusetts, Lowell. **SARAH KREPS** is an assistant professor of government at Cornell University.

A Day Job Waiting for a Kill Shot a World Away

BY ELISABETH BUMILLER | JULY 29, 2012

HANCOCK FIELD AIR NATIONAL GUARD BASE, N.Y. — From his computer console here in the Syracuse suburbs, Col. D. Scott Brenton remotely flies a Reaper drone that beams back hundreds of hours of live video of insurgents, his intended targets, going about their daily lives 7,000 miles away in Afghanistan. Sometimes he and his team watch the same family compound for weeks.

"I see mothers with children, I see fathers with children, I see fathers with mothers, I see kids playing soccer," Colonel Brenton said.

When the call comes for him to fire a missile and kill a militant — and only, Colonel Brenton said, when the women and children are not around — the hair on the back of his neck stands up, just as it did when he used to line up targets in his F-16 fighter jet.

Afterward, just like the old days, he compartmentalizes. "I feel no emotional attachment to the enemy," he said. "I have a duty, and I execute the duty."

Drones are not only revolutionizing American warfare but are also changing in profound ways the lives of the people who fly them.

Colonel Brenton acknowledges the peculiar new disconnect of fighting a telewar with a joystick and a throttle from his padded seat in American suburbia.

When he was deployed in Iraq, "you land and there's no more weapons on your F-16, people have an idea of what you were just involved with." Now he steps out of a dark room of video screens, his adrenaline still surging after squeezing the trigger, and commutes home past fast-food restaurants and convenience stores to help with homework — but always alone with what he has done.

"It's a strange feeling," he said. "No one in my immediate environment is aware of anything that occurred."

A drone pilot at the base at Hancock Field, near Syracuse, working the controls during a training operation.

Routinely thought of as robots that turn wars into sanitized video games, the drones have powerful cameras that bring war straight into a pilot's face.

Although pilots speak glowingly of the good days, when they can look at a video feed and warn a ground patrol in Afghanistan about an ambush ahead, the Air Force is also moving chaplains and medics just outside drone operation centers to help pilots deal with the bad days — images of a child killed in error or a close-up of a Marine shot in a raid gone wrong.

Among the toughest psychological tasks is the close surveillance for aerial sniper missions, reminiscent of the East German Stasi officer absorbed by the people he spies on in the movie "The Lives of Others." A drone pilot and his partner, a sensor operator who manipulates the aircraft's camera, observe the habits of a militant as he plays with his children, talks to his wife and visits his neighbors.

They then try to time their strike when, for example, his family is out at the market.

"They watch this guy do bad things and then his regular old life things," said Col. Hernando Ortega, the chief of aerospace medicine for the Air Education Training Command, who helped conduct a study last year on the stresses on drone pilots. "At some point, some of the stuff might remind you of stuff you did yourself. You might gain a level of familiarity that makes it a little difficult to pull the trigger."

Of a dozen pilots, sensor operators and supporting intelligence analysts recently interviewed from three American military bases, none acknowledged the kind of personal feelings for Afghans that would keep them awake at night after seeing the bloodshed left by missiles and bombs. But all spoke of a certain intimacy with Afghan family life that traditional pilots never see from 20,000 feet, and that even ground troops seldom experience.

"You see them wake up in the morning, do their work, go to sleep at night," said Dave, an Air Force major who flew drones from 2007 to 2009 at Creech Air Force Base in Nevada and now trains drone pilots at Holloman Air Force Base in New Mexico. (The Air Force, citing what it says are credible threats, forbids pilots to disclose their last names. Senior commanders who speak to the news media and community groups about the base's mission, like Colonel Brenton in Syracuse, use their full names.)

Some pilots spoke of the roiling emotions after they fire a missile. (Only pilots, all of them officers, employ weapons for strikes.)

"There was good reason for killing the people that I did, and I go through it in my head over and over and over," said Will, an Air Force officer who was a pilot at Creech and now trains others at Holloman. "But you never forget about it. It never just fades away, I don't think — not for me."

The complexities will only grow as the military struggles to keep up with a near insatiable demand for drones. The Air Force now has more than 1,300 drone pilots, about 300 less than it needs, stationed at 13 or more bases across the United States. They fly the unmanned aircraft mostly in Afghanistan. (The numbers do not include the classified program of the C.I.A., which conducts drone strikes in Pakistan, Somalia and Yemen.) Although the Afghan war is winding down, the military expects drones to help compensate for fewer troops on the ground.

By 2015, the Pentagon projects that the Air Force will need more than 2,000 drone pilots for combat air patrols operating 24 hours a day worldwide. The Air Force is already training more drone pilots — 350 last year — than fighter and bomber pilots combined. Until this year, drone pilots went through traditional flight training before learning how to operate Predators, Reapers and unarmed Global Hawks. Now the pilots are on a fast track and spend only 40 hours in a basic Cessna-type plane before starting their drone training.

Gen. Norton A. Schwartz, the Air Force chief of staff, said it was "conceivable" that drone pilots in the Air Force would outnumber those in cockpits in the foreseeable future, although he predicted that the Air Force would have traditional pilots for at least 30 more years.

Many drone pilots once flew in the air themselves but switched to drones out of a sense of the inevitable — or if they flew cargo planes, to feel closer to the war. "You definitely feel more connected to the guys, the battle," said Dave, the Air Force major, who flew C-130 transport planes in Iraq and Afghanistan.

Now more and more Air National Guard bases are abandoning traditional aircraft and switching to drones to meet demand, among them Hancock Field, which retired its F-16s and switched to Reapers in 2010. Colonel Brenton, who by then had logged more than 4,000 hours flying F-16s in 15 years of active duty and a decade in Syracuse deploying to war zones with the Guard, said he learned to fly drones to stay connected to combat. True, drones cannot engage in air-to-air combat, but Colonel Brenton said that "the amount of time I've engaged the enemy in air-to-ground combat has been significant" in both Reapers and F-16s.

"I feel like I'm doing the same thing I've always done, I just don't deploy to do it," he said. Now he works full time commanding a force of about 220 Reaper pilots, sensor operators and intelligence analysts at the base.

Pilots say the best days are when ground troops thank them for keeping them safe. Ted, an Air Force major and an F-16 pilot who flew Reapers from Creech, recalled how troops on an extended patrol away from their base in Afghanistan were grateful when he flew a Reaper above them for five hours so they could get some sleep one night. They told him, "We're keeping one guy awake to talk to you, but if you can, just watch over and make sure nobody's sneaking up on us," he recalled.

All the operators dismiss the notion that they are playing a video game. (They also reject the word "drone" because they say it describes an aircraft that flies on its own. They call their planes remotely piloted aircraft.)

"I don't have any video games that ask me to sit in one seat for six hours and look at the same target," said Joshua, a sensor operator who worked at Creech for a decade and is now a trainer at Holloman. "One of the things we try to beat into our crews is that this is a real aircraft with a real human component, and whatever decisions you make, good or bad, there's going to be actual consequences."

In his 10 years at Creech, he said without elaborating, "I've seen some pretty disturbing things."

All of the pilots who once flew in cockpits say they do miss the sensation of flight, which for Colonel Brenton extends to the F-16 flybys he did for the Syracuse Memorial Day parade downtown. To make up for it, he sometimes heads out on weekends in a small propeller plane, which he calls a bug smasher.

"It's nice to be up in the air," he said.

Let the Military Run Drone Warfare

OPINION | BY ADAM B. SCHIFF | MARCH 12, 2014

WASHINGTON — As night fell on what had been a scorching August day in Hadhramaut, Yemen, in 2012, four large explosions shattered the quiet. When the smoke cleared a few minutes later, Sheik Salem Ahmed bin Ali Jaber, a respected and openly anti-extremist cleric, his cousin, a young local police officer named Waleed Abdullah bin Ali Jaber, and three other men, who have been identified in news reports as likely extremists, lay dead — reportedly by an American drone strike.

Late last year I met Faisal bin Ali Jaber, a Yemeni civil engineer, and came face to face with the very real consequences of drone warfare. Faisal's brother-in-law Salem Jaber and nephew Waleed Jaber were two of the five people killed in the strike. Neither had any terrorist ties. It appears they were simply in the wrong place at the wrong time. Faisal's journey to the United States Capitol was a remarkable pilgrimage to share his family's anguish and to remind us of the human toll of the drone campaign that has been a feature of the war on Al Qaeda since the attacks of Sept. 11, 2001.

In a fight against a hidden enemy who operates in lawless safe havens, drones offer many obvious advantages and have taken many dangerous adversaries off the battlefield. But the idea that warfare can be precise, distant or sterile is also dangerous. It can easily blind us to the human cost of those inadvertently killed. And it can cause us to lose sight of the strategic imperative that we not multiply our enemies by causing the inadvertent loss of innocent lives.

There was precious little I could say to Faisal. What I did tell him was that, unlike the terrorists we target, America places a high value on the lives of innocent civilians. I also told him that our personnel make extraordinary efforts to ensure that civilians will not be killed or harmed by any strike. But I could not say whether anyone from the

United States government would ever be able to tell him just what had happened, or why.

It has been widely reported that the C.I.A. has been responsible for unmanned drone attacks. Last May, President Obama spoke at the National Defense University to articulate the legal and policy basis of the government's drone program, promising transparency and reform. But the single biggest reform — ensuring that only the Department of Defense carries out lethal strikes — remains stalled by Congressional opposition and bureaucratic inertia.

Those roadblocks must no longer stand in the way of reforms to increase the transparency, accountability and legitimacy of our drone program.

First, Congress needs to get out of the way and allow the president to move the drone program to the Joint Special Operations Command (J.S.O.C.) at the Pentagon. Though it may appear that we'd just be shuffling the chairs, this change would have two benefits: It would allow our other agencies to focus on their core mission of intelligence gathering, rather than paramilitary activities, and it would enable us to be more public about the successes and failures of the drone program, since such operations would no longer be covert.

Some Republicans and Democrats on both the House and Senate intelligence committees argue that the J.S.O.C. lacks expertise in targeting and may cause more collateral damage. But these claims are more anecdotal than evidentiary, and the intelligence committees have yet to be presented with the facts to back them up. They also ignore the joint role that Defense Department and intelligence agency personnel play in identifying and locating targets. These combined efforts would continue, even if the agency pulling the trigger changed.

Second, we must hold ourselves accountable by being more open about the effect of our drone strikes. While there may still be a need for covert drone operations in some parts of the world, greater disclosure would be in our interest. In the absence of official accounts, inflated and often wildly inaccurate assertions of the number of civilian casualties — generally advanced by our enemies — fill the informational vacuum. I've proposed legislation, along with my fellow California Democrat Senator Dianne Feinstein, to require an annual report of the number of civilian and combatant casualties caused by drone strikes, including an explanation of how we define those terms.

Finally, with regard to the uniquely difficult situation of an American citizen who has taken up arms against his own nation and who cannot feasibly be arrested, the Obama administration must go further to explain what protections are in place to ensure due process for any American who may be targeted. A 2011 strike targeted and killed Anwar al-Awlaki, an American-born cleric and top operative of Al Qaeda's branch in Yemen, and other Americans may be targeted in the future. I've put forward a proposal to require an independent review of any decision to target an American with lethal force. These reports should be declassified after 10 years. Knowing that they'll be made public will help ensure that the task is approached with the appropriate rigor.

The United States is the only country with a significant armed drone capability, but that distinction will not last forever. As other nations develop and deploy these technologies, we will be better positioned to urge their responsible and transparent use if we have set an example ourselves. We must hold ourselves to a high standard and do it in public, not behind closed doors.

That is the commitment the president has made, and it's a promise worth keeping.

ADAM B. SCHIFF, Democrat of California, is a member of the House Permanent Select Committee on Intelligence.

New Rules Set on Armed Drone Exports

BY SCOTT SHANE | FEB. 17, 2015

WASHINGTON — The Obama administration on Tuesday issued new rules for the international export of armed drones, a move that seeks to preserve an American lead in a fast-growing market but one likely to speed the proliferation of a much-criticized weapon in the battle against terrorism.

The rules will make it easier to provide missile-armed Predator and Reaper drones to American allies facing off against militant groups, including the Islamic State and its offshoots, aviation experts said. The long-awaited policy shift will reduce the chance that friendly countries will turn for drones to Israel or China, which also manufacture unmanned military aircraft for export.

The State Department said the new policy set strict standards for the sale of armed drones, including "end-use assurances" from the recipient countries that set out how they can be used. For drones capable of carrying large weapons, there will be a "strong presumption of denial" of an export license. But exceptions will be allowed on "rare occasions," the department said, citing language that also governs other weapons exports.

The export rules will not permit buyers to use American drones "to conduct unlawful surveillance or use unlawful force against their domestic populations," the State Department said.

The new policy is a recognition that unmanned aircraft are increasingly viewed around the globe as an indispensable weapon for counterterrorism and warfare. To date, experts said, the United States has sold armed drones only to Britain, though several NATO countries have bought unarmed models.

Italy has sought approval to add missiles to its American-made drones, and Turkey has also sought to buy armed American unmanned craft.

Human rights groups have expressed grave concern about drone proliferation because they say the ability to strike without risking a pilot's life lowers the threshold for starting an armed conflict. In addition, though drones have a far greater capability to distinguish between civilians and combatants than fighter jets or cruise missiles, American drones in Pakistan and Yemen have killed hundreds of civilians.

Peter W. Singer, an expert on robotic weaponry at the New America Foundation, said the new rules filled a policy vacuum that had lasted for years.

"The reality is that the technology is here to stay, and it's globally proliferating," he said. "So to have a policy is a good thing."

But he said that, as with other arms exports, American-made armed drones that are exported are likely to be used for dubious or regrettable purposes.

"Whether it's an F-16, an armed drone or a billy club, once you sell it to another country, you lose control over how it's used," Mr. Singer said.

Eric R. McClafferty, a lawyer at Kelley Drye & Warren who specializes in export controls, said there had been intense pressure from American industry to permit the export of both military and nonmilitary drones. That is in part because unmanned aircraft are viewed as a growth area by defense manufacturers.

"You have tons of allies who really want these UAVs," he said, referring to unmanned aerial vehicles.

Mr. McClafferty suggested that the Obama administration was now addressing the proliferation of all kinds of drones, from the tiny models popular with hobbyists and photographers to the military models. On Sunday, the Federal Aviation Administration issued new rules governing the commercial use of small drones inside the United States.

Philip Finnegan, director of corporate analysis at the Teal Group, which tracks the aviation industry, said there was currently a global market for unmanned aircraft of about $6 billion a year. Only a tiny fraction of that is for armed drones, he said, but the share is growing fast.

While the United States, Israel and China dominate the field, South Africa is now making armed drones, and Turkey and several other countries are in the early stages of developing military models, Mr. Finnegan said. Russia has lagged so far, he said.

While the first unmanned aircraft date almost to the origins of aviation, the Predator drone was armed with missiles after the Sept. 11, 2001, attacks with the goal of killing Osama bin Laden and other terrorists. The weapon has been seen as particularly well-adapted for use in counterterrorism, because it can kill a small number of people with precision when all goes well.

Since 2001, the United States has used drones for surveillance and strikes in Afghanistan, Iraq, Pakistan, Somalia and Yemen, and both military and C.I.A. officials have praised their capabilities.

But strikes can be only as precise as the intelligence that guides them, and in numerous cases, missiles fired from drones have hit the wrong people or killed and injured nearby civilians. The result has been a potent political backlash, particularly in Pakistan and Yemen, which Al Qaeda and other militants have used as a recruiting gambit.

CHAPTER 3

Doubts and Pushback Raise Questions

As heavy drone use continued into President Obama's second term, critics of the program and journalists alike began to question the accuracy of statistics released by the U.S. government. It also became clear that some terrorists were conducting attacks because of the drone program itself. Even with government assurances and extended military honors for drone pilots, experts and human rights groups remained vocally opposed to drone warfare. Were precise drone strikes killing precisely the wrong people? As the only country with substantial armed drone capability, was this too much power for the United States? Did the gains truly outweigh the loss of innocent civilian life?

Drone Strikes Reveal Uncomfortable Truth: U.S. Is Often Unsure About Who Will Die

BY SCOTT SHANE | APRIL 23, 2015

BARACK OBAMA INHERITED two ugly, intractable wars in Iraq and Afghanistan when he became president and set to work to end them. But a third, more covert war he made his own, escalating drone strikes in Pakistan and expanding them to Yemen and Somalia.

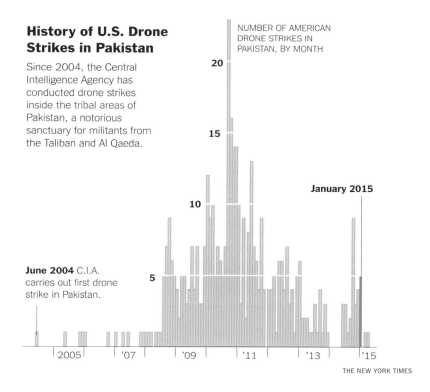

History of U.S. Drone Strikes in Pakistan

Since 2004, the Central Intelligence Agency has conducted drone strikes inside the tribal areas of Pakistan, a notorious sanctuary for militants from the Taliban and Al Qaeda.

NUMBER OF AMERICAN DRONE STRIKES IN PAKISTAN, BY MONTH

20

15

January 2015

10

June 2004 C.I.A. carries out first drone strike in Pakistan.

5

2005   '07   '09   '11   '13   '15

THE NEW YORK TIMES

The drone's vaunted capability for pinpoint killing appealed to a president intrigued by a new technology and determined to try to keep the United States out of new quagmires. Aides said Mr. Obama liked the idea of picking off dangerous terrorists a few at a time, without endangering American lives or risking the yearslong bloodshed of conventional war.

"Let's kill the people who are trying to kill us," he often told aides.

By most accounts, hundreds of dangerous militants have, indeed, been killed by drones, including some high-ranking Qaeda figures. But for six years, when the heavy cloak of secrecy has occasionally been breached, the results of some strikes have often turned out to be deeply troubling.

Every independent investigation of the strikes has found far more civilian casualties than administration officials admit. Gradually, it has become clear that when operators in Nevada fire missiles into remote tribal territories on the other side of the world, they often do not know who they are killing, but are making an imperfect best guess.

The president's announcement on Thursday that a January strike on Al Qaeda in Pakistan had killed two Western hostages, and that it took many weeks to confirm their deaths, bolstered the assessments of the program's harshest outside critics. The dark picture was compounded by the additional disclosure that two American members of Al Qaeda were killed in strikes that same month, but neither had been identified in advance and deliberately targeted.

In all, it was a devastating acknowledgment for Mr. Obama, who had hoped to pioneer a new, more discriminating kind of warfare. Whether the episode might bring a long-delayed public reckoning about targeted killings, long hidden by classification rules, remained uncertain.

Even some former Obama administration security officials have expressed serious doubts about the wisdom of the program, given the ire it has ignited overseas and the terrorists who have said they plotted attacks because of drones. And outside experts have long called for a candid accounting of the results of strikes.

"I hope this event allows us at last to have an honest dialogue about the U.S. drone program," said Rachel Stohl, of the Stimson Center, a Washington research institute. "These are precise weapons. The failure is in the intelligence about who it is that we are killing."

Ms. Stohl noted that Mr. Obama and his top aides have repeatedly promised greater openness about the drone program but have never really delivered on it.

In a speech in 2013 about drones, Mr. Obama declared that no strike was taken without "near-certainty that no civilians will be killed or injured." He added that "nevertheless, it is a hard fact that U.S. strikes have resulted in civilian casualties" and said "those deaths will haunt us as long as we live."

But over the Obama presidency, it has become harder for journalists to obtain information from the government on the results of particular strikes. And Mr. Obama's Justice Department has fought in court for years to keep secret the legal opinions justifying strikes.

Micah Zenko, a scholar at the Council on Foreign Relations and lead author of a 2013 study of drones, said the president's statement "highlights what we've sort of known: that most individuals killed are not on a kill list, and the government does not know their names."

Mr. Zenko noted that with the new disclosures, a total of eight Americans have been killed in drone strikes. Of those, only one, the American cleric Anwar al-Awlaki, who joined Al Qaeda in Yemen and was killed in 2011, was identified and deliberately targeted. The rest were killed in strikes aimed at other militants, or in so-called signature strikes based on indications that people on the ground were likely with Al Qaeda or allied militant groups.

Though by most accounts six of the eight Americans were allied with Al Qaeda, Obama administration lawyers have ruled that a special legal review should be conducted before killing Americans suspected of terrorism. Such a review, they have argued, amounts to the legal "due process" required by the Constitution, though some legal scholars do not believe such reviews meet the constitutional test.

When Americans have been killed, however, the Obama administration has found it necessary to break with its usual practice and eventually acknowledge the deaths, at least in private discussions with reporters.

That was the case in the first C.I.A. drone strike, in Yemen in 2002, which turned out to have killed an American in Al Qaeda. It was the case in 2011, when an American Qaeda propagandist from North Carolina, Samir Khan, was killed along with Mr. Awlaki. And it happened two weeks later, when another American strike killed Mr. Awlaki's 16-year-old son and his 17-year-old cousin.

Military and intelligence officials said they did not know that the teenagers were present when they took a shot at a Qaeda operative who, it turned out, was not there. But such admissions, in the rare cases that officials were willing to discuss, undercut their argument that in most cases they were confident that they were killing only dangerous militants.

Most security experts still believe that drones, which allow a scene to be watched for hours or days through video feeds, still offer at least the chance of greater accuracy than other means of killing terrorists. By most accounts, conventional airstrikes and ground invasions kill a higher proportion of noncombatants. But without detailed, reliable, on-the-ground intelligence, experience has shown, drones make it possible to precisely kill the wrong people.

Mr. Zenko said that an average of separate counts of American drone strikes by three organizations, the New America Foundation, the Bureau of Investigative Journalism and The Long War Journal, finds that 522 strikes have killed 3,852 people, 476 of them civilians. But those counts, based on news accounts and some on-the-ground interviews, are considered very rough estimates.

The proliferating mistakes have given drones a sinister reputation in Pakistan and Yemen and have provoked a powerful anti-American backlash in the Muslim world. Part of the collateral damage in the strikes has been Mr. Obama's dream of restoring the United States' reputation with Muslims around the globe.

Despite the bad reviews overseas, drone strikes remain persistently popular with the American public, with about two-thirds expressing approval in polls. And despite the protests of a few liberal Democrats or libertarian Republicans, they have enjoyed unusual bipartisan support in Congress, where they are viewed as reducing the threat of terrorist attack and keeping American operators out of harm's way.

Mr. Zenko said that Mr. Obama and Congress should create a commission to examine the targeted killing program, its results and its flaws. But he said the combination of public and Congressional popularity probably mean that even the latest disclosures will not bring such scrutiny to the program.

"I predict that even this episode will have no effect," he said.

MATT APUZZO and **MATTHEW ROSENBERG** contributed reporting.

'Drone' Documentary Examines a New Weapon

REVIEW | BY NEIL GENZLINGER | NOV. 19, 2015

THIS PROBABLY ISN'T the best moment to find a receptive audience for a film that questions the American use of drone strikes in the war on terror. Regardless of whether armed drones would have been useful countering the attacks in Paris, those events have many people locked into a "whatever it takes" mentality when it comes to fighting extremism.

But "Drone," a documentary by the Norwegian filmmaker Tonje Hessen Schei, has a lot to say that needs to be heard. Some of it is already fairly familiar, though that makes it no less urgent. The morality of killing people without trial and the substantial civilian casualties caused by the so-called targeted strikes have been the source of debate and protest for some time. And others have argued, as this film does, that drone warfare is actually a recruitment tool for terrorist groups because of the resentment it is generating.

But this film examines some less familiar issues, too, including how the makers of traditional weapons will respond as the increasing use of drones reduces demand for heavy armaments. There is also a chilling nod to the fact that drones aren't the exclusive province of the United States or its allies.

Col. Lawrence Wilkerson, chief of staff to Colin Powell when he was secretary of state, says, "There has never been any technology of warfare that isn't ultimately adopted by your enemy or enemies." Then comes an aerial shot of Lower Manhattan.

There are no suggested solutions here to the difficult issues raised, but the film at least reminds us that it's important not to accept this new way of warring without scrutinizing it.

Pentagon Will Extend Military Honors to Drone Operators Far From Battles

BY MICHAEL S. SCHMIDT | JAN. 6, 2016

WASHINGTON — For years, the military's drone pilots have toiled in obscurity from windowless rooms at bases in suburban America, viewed by some in the armed forces more as video game players than as warriors.

But in a reflection of their increasingly important role under President Obama, the drone operators will now be eligible for military honors akin to those given to pilots who flew over the battlefields of Iraq and Afghanistan.

The Defense Department on Thursday is scheduled to announce that it has created a designation to recognize service members who had a direct effect on combat operations even though they were operating remotely, Pentagon officials said. Drone pilots are likely to receive many of the awards, but they may also be given to operators who launch cyberattacks.

"It's way past time," said David A. Deptula, a retired three-star Air Force general who pushed the military to embrace drones. "People should be acknowledged and rewarded for their contributions to accomplishing security objections regardless of where they are located."

Current and former military officials had been deeply divided about whether to recognize the drone pilots. An initial Pentagon plan in 2013 to honor them with a "Distinguished Warfare Medal" was criticized by some veterans' groups, which feared that the award would rank higher than combat medals like the Bronze Star and the Purple Heart.

The Veterans of Foreign Wars sent a letter to Mr. Obama expressing its objections to the proposed medal. Some veterans have derided such recognition as a "geek cross." Defense Secretary Leon E. Panetta announced the planned medal during his final days at the Pentagon in 2013.

But the proposal was scuttled by his successor, Chuck Hagel, amid the fury from the veterans' groups.

The Pentagon's efforts to recognize service members who operate from afar reflect the changing nature of how the military uses force. With the American public weary of war, Mr. Obama has relied on drones as the military has moved toward a leaner footprint in its engagements in Iraq, Afghanistan, Pakistan and Yemen.

"As the impact of remote operations on combat continues to increase, the necessity of ensuring those actions are distinctly recognized grows," said a Pentagon document outlining changes to how the military gives awards and other decorations.

The use of drones has been widely credited with diminishing Al Qaeda and other terrorist groups. But civilians have also died in drone attacks, fueling anger toward the United States among Muslims across the Middle East.

The military has also increased its use of cyberweapons. In 2010, a cyberattack took out nearly 1,000 centrifuges that Iran had been using to purify uranium.

The new awards, a Pentagon official said, will allow the military to recognize service members who operate other technology that will be developed in the future as military tactics evolve.

The Pentagon is also planning to make changes that officials hope will shorten the time that it takes to award the Medal of Honor, and to standardize what define "acts of combat valor."

Along with those changes, Defense Secretary Ashton B. Carter is scheduled to announce a review of how Silver Star and Service Cross medals have been awarded for combat in the wars in Iraq and Afghanistan. The review will examine whether the standards for earning those medals have remained the same throughout the years since the wars began, and it could result in upgrades for some service members.

According to the Pentagon, the first seven Medal of Honor awards for service in Iraq and Afghanistan were given to those who had died.

But since 2010, all 10 people who have received the Medal of Honor have been living at the time it was awarded.

Some commanders have been more willing to upgrade their recommendations for medals as the wars dragged on, according to Pentagon officials. So some service members could receive upgraded honors for actions that took place early in those conflicts.

Limit the Next President's Power to Wage Drone Warfare

OPINION | BY JAMEEL JAFFER AND BRETT MAX KAUFMAN | MARCH 8, 2016

WHEN BARACK OBAMA took office as the reluctant heir to George W. Bush's "war on terror," he renounced some of his predecessor's most extreme policies. There is one Bush-era policy, though, that President Obama made emphatically his own: the summary killing of suspected militants and terrorists, usually by drone.

In less than a year, the president will bequeath this policy, and the sweeping legal claims that underlie it, to someone who may see the world very differently from him. Before that happens, he should bring the drone campaign out of the shadows and do what he can to constrain the power he unleashed.

President Bush started the drone wars, but Mr. Obama vastly expanded them. Almost entirely on his watch, United States strikes have killed as many as 5,000 people, possibly 1,000 of them civilians. The president approved strikes in places far from combat zones. He authorized the C.I.A. to carry out "signature strikes" aimed at people whose identities the agency did not know but whose activities supposedly suggested militancy. He approved the deliberate killing of an American, Anwar al-Awlaki.

The president also oversaw an aggressive effort to control the public narrative about drone strikes. Even as senior officials selectively disclosed information to the news media, his administration resisted Freedom of Information Act lawsuits, arguing that national security would be harmed if the government confirmed drone strikes were taking place.

The administration also argued in court that federal judges lacked the authority to say whether drone strikes were lawful. It refused to release the evidence that it claimed made Mr. Awlaki a lawful target. In lieu of information, the administration offered assurances that the president and his aides were deeply moral people who agonized over authorizing lethal force.

But as this election season has underscored, powers this far-reaching should not rest solely on the character of the president and his advisers. In a democracy, the ability to use lethal force must be subject to clear and narrow limits, and the public must be able to evaluate whether those limits are being respected. Mr. Obama observed almost three years ago that "the same human progress that gives us the technology to strike half a world away also demands the discipline to constrain that power." At the very least, the president has the responsibility to ensure that drone strikes are subject to meaningful oversight.

The president should begin by publishing the Presidential Policy Guidance, a document that has provided the legal and administrative framework for the drone campaign since 2013. In response to litigation, the administration informed a federal judge last week that it would release parts of the document, but it remains to be seen how extensive the disclosure will be and whether it will be accompanied by a broader reconsideration of the secrecy surrounding the program.

The president should also release the legal memos that purport to justify drone strikes away from battlefields. Courts have compelled the administration to release portions of two of these memos, but the public should have access to all of the government's legal reasoning about who may be targeted, where and for what reasons. The government has a legitimate interest in protecting properly classified information, but the law behind the drone program should not be a secret.

The president should also make it the country's default practice to acknowledge all drone strikes — not just those carried out on conventional battlefields, as in Iraq and Syria. To facilitate this shift toward greater transparency and to strengthen congressional oversight, he should withdraw the C.I.A.'s authority to carry out drone strikes and provide that any future strikes will be authorized and carried out by the Department of Defense.

On Monday, the president's chief counterterrorism adviser said that the government intended to disclose annual assessments of casualties from lethal strikes "outside areas of active hostilities." This information will be of limited use to the public, however, unless the government also discloses information about individual strikes — when and where they took place, and numbers of casualties.

Finally, the president should establish a policy of investigating and publicly explaining strikes that kill innocent civilians, and of compensating those victims' families. After an American drone strike last year killed two Western hostages, Warren Weinstein and Giovanni Lo Porto, the government apologized, opened an investigation and said it would offer compensation. It should do the same when drone strikes kill or maim innocent Pakistanis, Yemenis and Somalis.

These kinds of changes, of course, will not quiet the drone campaign's critics. Many of those critics believe, as we do, that the campaign is broader than international law permits, that congressional oversight should be far more stringent and that, at least in some circumstances, the lawfulness of strikes should be subject to after-the-fact review by the courts.

But at a minimum, the changes we propose would allow for a more informed debate about a subject that urgently needs one, and they would create new, if modest, checks against overreach and abuse. Equally important, the president could make the changes we propose on his own in the limited time he has left in office.

President Obama has established a dangerous precedent, and consequently whoever prevails in November will inherit a sweeping power to use lethal force against suspected terrorists and militants, including Americans. The new president, whether a Democrat or a Republican, should also inherit policies that limit that power.

JAMEEL JAFFER is deputy legal director of the American Civil Liberties Union.
BRETT MAX KAUFMAN is a staff lawyer in the A.C.L.U.'s Center for Democracy.

Drone Strike Statistics Answer Few Questions, and Raise Many

BY SCOTT SHANE | JULY 3, 2016

WASHINGTON — The promise of the armed drone has always been precision: The United States could kill just the small number of dangerous terrorists it wanted to kill, leaving nearby civilians unharmed.

But the Obama administration's unprecedented release last week of statistics on counterterrorism strikes underscored how much more complicated the results of the drone program have been.

It showed that even inside the government, there is no certainty about whom it has killed. And it highlighted the skepticism with which official American claims on targeted killing are viewed by human rights groups and independent experts, including those who believe the strikes have eliminated some very dangerous people.

"It's an important step — it's an acknowledgment that transparency is needed," said Rachel Stohl, an author of two studies of the drone program and a senior associate at the Stimson Center, a research group in Washington. "But I don't feel like we have enough information to analyze whether this tactic is working and helping us achieve larger strategic aims."

More broadly, President Obama's move to open a window on the secret counterterrorism program takes place against a background of escalating jihadist violence that can be called up by a list of cities that includes Paris; San Bernardino, Calif.; Brussels; Orlando, Fla.; Kabul, Afghanistan; Istanbul; Baghdad; and now Dhaka, Bangladesh.

Apart from the dispute over the number of civilian deaths, the notion that targeted drone strikes are an adequate answer to the terrorist threat appears increasingly threadbare.

"There's a massive failure of strategy," said Akbar S. Ahmed, a former Pakistani diplomat and the chairman of Islamic studies at American University in Washington. Drones have simply become one more

Monitoring Air Force drone footage from Afghanistan in 2010.

element of the violence in countries like Pakistan and Yemen, not a way to reduce violence, he said.

Among young people attracted to jihadist ideology, "the line to blow yourself up remains horrifyingly long," he said. "That line should be getting shorter."

A senior Obama administration official, who spoke on the condition of anonymity to discuss the classified program, said the recent series of major terror attacks in urban areas had all been directed or inspired by the Islamic State.

The classified counterterrorism drone campaign, he said, has targeted other groups, notably Al Qaeda's old core in Pakistan, its branch in Yemen and the Shabab in Somalia. (Because the strikes in Pakistan are a covert action program, the official was not per- mitted to name that country.) No attack in the West in the past year has been traced to those groups, suggesting that the strikes have been effective, he said. The drone strikes in Iraq, Syria and

Afghanistan are, for the most part, carried out by the military in a separate program.

In Friday's release, the White House made public an executive order laying out policies to minimize civilian casualties in counterterrorism strikes and a plan to start making public the basic statistics on strikes each year.

At the same time, the Office of the Director of National Intelligence released the first official estimates of those killed during Mr. Obama's presidency in strikes outside the conventional wars in Iraq, Syria and Afghanistan. Though the announcement did not say so, the classified strikes took place in Libya, Pakistan, Somalia and Yemen, and the vast majority used missiles fired from unmanned drone aircraft, though a few used piloted jets or cruise missiles fired from the sea.

Since 2009, the government said, 473 strikes had killed between 2,372 and 2,581 combatants. They are defined as members of groups, like Al Qaeda and the Taliban, that are considered to be at war with the United States, or others posing a "continuing and imminent threat" to Americans.

In the most sharply debated statistics, the statement estimated that between 64 and 116 noncombatants had been killed. Officials said those numbers included both clearly innocent civilians and others for whom there was insufficient evidence to be sure they were combatants.

The numbers were far lower than previous estimates from the three independent organizations that track strikes based on news reports and other sources. The Long War Journal, whose estimates are lowest, counted 207 civilian deaths in Pakistan and Yemen alone. The security policy group New America in Washington estimated a minimum of 216 in those two countries, and the London-based Bureau of Investigative Journalism estimated the civilian toll under Mr. Obama between 380 and 801.

With no breakdown by year or country, let alone a detailed strike-by-strike account, the Obama administration's new data was difficult to assess. For example, according to multiple studies by Human Rights

Watch, Yemen's Parliament and others, an American cruise missile strike in Yemen on Dec. 17, 2009, killed 41 civilians, including 22 children and a dozen women. At least three more people were killed later after handling unexploded cluster munitions left from the strike.

If those 41 are included in the new official count, as appears likely, that would leave only 23 civilians killed in all other strikes since 2009 to reach the low-end American estimate of 64. By nearly all independent accounts, that number is implausibly low. Obama administration officials declined over the weekend to discuss any specific strikes or otherwise elaborate on the statistics.

Scott F. Murray, who retired from the Air Force as a colonel after 29 years, was a career intelligence officer involved in overseeing airstrikes in Iraq, Afghanistan and Syria. He said that while he had not been involved directly in the counterterrorist strikes outside those war zones, the civilian death estimates were "lower than I would have expected."

He said civilian deaths could result from multiple causes, including incomplete intelligence about the identities of people on the ground, equipment failure and human error.

Perhaps most often, Mr. Murray said, problems arise when civilians enter a target area before drone surveillance begins, or when a civilian suddenly enters the strike zone just before a strike.

"The night you choose to strike, it may be that the in-laws arrived earlier in the day or the children's birthday party is ongoing and you weren't watching when everyone arrived," Mr. Murray said. "Those are the things in war that drive you to drink. You never ever have perfect information."

Brandon Bryant, who worked on Air Force drone teams from 2006 to 2011 and has become an outspoken critic of the program, recalled one strike in 2007 targeting a local Taliban commander. As the Hellfire missile sped toward the small house, he said, a small child — possibly frightened by the missile's sonic boom — ran into the house and was killed.

"Those things are burned into my brain — I can't really forget them," Mr. Bryant said. He added that he believed total civilian deaths were much higher than the administration's estimate because of officials' wishful thinking, rather than deliberate deception. "They're just deluding themselves about the impact," he said.

The senior administration official acknowledged the fear and frustration produced by the recent urban attacks and said Mr. Obama's strategy went far beyond drone strikes, incorporating the military battle against the Islamic State in Iraq and Syria, counter-messaging against jihadist groups, and support for allies facing the same enemies as the United States.

American officials strongly defend the necessity of targeted killing, and the president's executive order suggests that he believes the drone program will endure far beyond his presidency. But deaths from terrorism have risen sharply since 2011, according to the Global Terrorism Index, compiled annually by researchers, and there is worry inside and outside the government that the United States and its allies are winning battles but losing the ideological war.

Of particular concern is the possibility that the rash of attacks carried out in the name of the Islamic State is just the beginning — not because the group is getting stronger but because it is getting weaker. As the United States and its allies uproot the Islamic State in Syria and Iraq, its supporters may turn to terrorism wherever they are, many terrorism experts believe. In most of those places, like the cities hit hardest in recent months, no drone strikes will be possible.

U.S. Release Rules for Airstrike Killings of Terror Suspects

BY CHARLIE SAVAGE | AUG. 6, 2016

WASHINGTON — The Obama administration has disclosed its rules and procedures for targeting individuals for killing outside conventional war zones — including with drones — further lifting the secrecy surrounding one of its most disputed tactics for fighting terrorism.

The newly declassified document shows that if the top lawyers and leaders of the departments and agencies on the National Security Council agree that a proposed strike would be lawful and appropriate, the Pentagon or the Central Intelligence Agency can proceed.

If they disagree, or if the person to be targeted is an American citizen, the matter must go to the president for a decision.

President Obama issued the 18-page set of rules, sometimes called the drone strike "playbook" but formally known as the Presidential Policy Guidance, in May 2013. It was classified, although the administration publicly said it tightened standards for strikes — including requirements that targets must pose a threat to Americans and the "near certainty" that there would be no civilian deaths.

The government had said this year that it intended to make the guidance public as part of a Freedom of Information Act lawsuit brought by the American Civil Liberties Union. It provided the document to the A.C.L.U. late Friday, and the organization posted it on its website Saturday morning.

"From one perspective it might be seen as reassuring, because it makes clear that these decisions are considered by many different senior people," Jameel Jaffer of the A.C.L.U. said. "On the other hand, the document drives home how bureaucraticized, and therefore normalized, this practice of killing people away from conventional battlefields has become."

Ned Price, a National Security Council spokesman, said in a statement Saturday, "The president has emphasized that the U.S. government should be as transparent as possible with the American people about our counterterrorism operations, the manner in which they are conducted and their results."

He added, "Our counterterrorism actions are effective and legal, and their legitimacy is best demonstrated by making public more information about these actions as well as setting clear standards for other nations to follow."

The release joins the disclosure last month of previously classified statistics showing the government's official count of the number of combatants and civilian bystanders killed in airstrikes where American troops are not engaged in regular combat. These places include the tribal areas of Pakistan as well as Somalia, Yemen and Libya.

The official death toll was significantly lower than estimates by independent groups that try to track such operations. And the government statistics did not break down bystander death numbers by year, so it was not possible to analyze the effects of Mr. Obama's 2013 changes, although the frequency of such airstrikes has dropped.

Airstrikes away from conventional battlefields, using both piloted aircraft and remotely operated drones, began to escalate toward the end of the George W. Bush administration and became a central counterterrorism tactic in Mr. Obama's first term.

It also attracted growing controversy among human rights groups as reports of civilian casualties soared in Pakistan and Yemen, and as the administration took the unprecedented step of targeting and killing an American citizen, Anwar al-Awlaki, without a trial. Mr. Awlaki, a New Mexico-born radical cleric accused of playing an operational role in terrorist plots by Al Qaeda's Yemen branch, was killed in a September 2011 drone strike.

In 2012, the president directed his administration to tighten procedures and standards, resulting in his May 2013 Presidential Policy Guidance and a major national security speech at National Defense University.

The framework of the procedures that emerged from that effort had been previously reported, but the reports relied on accounts from current and former officials. Now, with some redactions, the guidance itself has been made public, confirming those accounts and filling in gaps.

It shows, for example, that the operational agencies of the National Security Council — meaning the Defense Department and the C.I.A. — may nominate someone for proposed killing after a review by their top lawyers.

The National Counterterrorism Center then develops a report analyzing the intelligence about that person, and top lawyers across different security agencies deliberate over whether the person meets legal standards for attack.

The process then goes to the "deputies committee," made up of the No. 2 officials at national security departments and agencies. They weigh such factors as whether it is feasible to halt the perceived threat short of killing a terror suspect, and the impact of a strike on "the broader regional and international political interests of the United States."

The deputies make recommendations to their agency directors or department secretaries, who make up the "principals committee." If they unanimously agree — and if the target is not an American citizen — the strike can proceed with notice to the president. Otherwise, the president must make the decision.

But the document also says the president may waive the rules in "extraordinary cases." It cites when there is a "fleeting opportunity" and no time to follow the full review procedures, or a proposal to kill a suspect who "poses a continuing, imminent threat to another country's persons."

The guidance shows that in the case of a capture, rather than the killing of a terror suspect, the administration generally prefers to let other countries handle detention. If that is unworkable, the United States will take custody and try to prosecute the suspect, it says, but adds, "In no event will additional detainees be brought to the detention facilities at the Guantánamo Bay Naval Base."

CHAPTER 4

International Attention and Relations Intensify

As the Trump administration took office, concerns about drone use intensified in the international community. Strikes had already been conducted in Libya, Pakistan, Somalia and Yemen, among other countries, for years. The international perception of any moral authority the United States possessed was changing, due in part to President Trump's relaxation of the limitations on who qualified as a potential target for drone strikes. Jihadist foot-soldiers became just as likely targets as high-level terrorist leaders, despite the advice of national security experts.

U.S. Demands Return of Drone Seized by Chinese Warship

BY HELENE COOPER | DEC. 16, 2016

WASHINGTON — The Pentagon on Friday demanded the return of an underwater drone that was seized by China as an American crew was moving in to retrieve it. The episode threatens to increase tensions in a region already fraught with great-power rivalries.

A Chinese warship had been shadowing the Bowditch, a United States naval vessel, in the international waters of the South China Sea when the Chinese launched a small boat and snatched the unmanned underwater vehicle, the Pentagon said.

Ignoring radio demands from the Americans to return the drone, the Chinese ship sailed off.

The episode set off one of the tensest standoffs between Beijing and Washington in 15 years and occurred a day after the Chinese signaled that they had installed weapons along a string of disputed islands in the South China Sea.

The seizure of the drone brought a formal protest from the United States at a time when China is extending claims over the South China Sea and is watching the United States — and its incoming president — with wariness.

The episode did not have the life-or-death drama of the April 2001 midair collision between a Chinese fighter jet and a Navy surveillance plane that forced the Americans to make an emergency landing on Chinese territory. Acknowledging the odd nature of Chinese sailors seizing the drone close to its American mother ship, one official here likened it to watching a thief steal a wallet in broad daylight.

American officials said they were still trying to determine whether the seizure was a low-level action taken by Chinese sailors who spotted the drone — which the Pentagon said was conducting scientific research — or a strategic-level action ordered by more senior Chinese leaders to challenge the American presence in those waters.

"We call upon China to return" the underwater vehicle "immediately," Peter Cook, the Pentagon press secretary, said in a statement Friday, "and to comply with all of its obligations under international law."

The incident complicates already testy relations between China and the United States, ties that have been further frayed by President-elect Donald J. Trump's phone call with the president of Taiwan. Mr. Trump angered Chinese officials by holding a phone conversation with President Tsai Ing-wen of Taiwan, an island that Beijing deems a breakaway province of China. It had been nearly four decades since a United States president or president-elect had such direct contact with a Taiwanese leader.

In an interview broadcast on Sunday, Mr. Trump also criticized China over its trade imbalance with the United States, its military activities in the South China Sea and its links to North Korea. Aides to the president-elect have defended Mr. Trump's words and actions as important to bringing a fresh eye to a number of foreign policy issues.

Pentagon officials said on Friday that they were trying to determine if the seizure of the underwater drone had anything to do with Mr. Trump's comments.

At the White House on Friday, President Obama was asked about the issue during a news conference, and he made clear that he viewed the question of Taiwan as especially sensitive. While the president refrained from directly criticizing Mr. Trump, he warned his successor to carefully consider his actions and any new policy, lest he ignite what could be a significant response from Beijing.

"I think all of our foreign policy should be subject to fresh eyes," Mr. Obama said. But he added: "For China, the issue of Taiwan is as important as anything on their docket. The idea of a One China is at the heart of their conception of a nation."

"And so if you are going to upend this understanding, you have to have thought through what the consequences are, because the Chinese will not treat that the way they'll treat other issues," he said, adding that the Chinese would not even treat it the way they treated issues around the South China Sea, "where we've had a lot of tensions."

China experts said on Friday that it was unclear whether the seizure of the American drone was linked to anger in Beijing over Mr. Trump, or a continuation of years of tensions over competing claims in the South China Sea.

The Bowditch episode came after China signaled on Thursday that it had installed weapons on disputed islands in the South China Sea that it would use to repel threats. In describing the new weapons deployment, a Defense Ministry statement suggested that China was further watering down a pledge made by its president, Xi Jinping, to not militarize the islands.

That indicated that such installations were part of China's plan to deepen its territorial claim over the islands, which has created tensions with its neighbors over their rival claims and with Washington over freedom of navigation in the South China Sea, one of the world's busiest commercial waterways. The United States Navy routinely sends warships to sail the South China Sea as part of ongoing American policy meant to demonstrate that all countries have the freedom of navigation in disputed waters.

M. Taylor Fravel, an associate professor of political science at M.I.T. who studies China's territorial disputes and has written on the South China Sea, called the seizure of the drone "a big deal, as it represents the deliberate theft of U.S. government property and a clear violation" of maritime law.

"By stealing a drone versus threatening the safety of the ship, China may be trying to find a way to signal its opposition to U.S. activities without creating a larger incident," Mr. Fravel said. "Nevertheless, it will be viewed by the U.S. as a clear challenge."

The Bowditch, an oceanographic ship, was operating in international waters and carrying out scientific research, said Capt. Jeff Davis, a Pentagon spokesman. The drone was part of an unclassified program to collect oceanographic data, including salinity in the sea, clarity of water and ocean temperature, factors that can help the military in its collection of sonar data.

The Chinese Navy ship, which had been shadowing the American ship, approached within 500 yards of the Bowditch before seizing the drone, which American officials say was around 50 nautical miles northwest of Subic Bay, the Philippines.

Whatever the case, the Pentagon said that China had no right to seize the drone. "This is not the sort of conduct we expect from professional navies," Captain Davis said.

Michael Swaine, a senior fellow at the Carnegie Endowment for International Peace, called the theft "low-level provocation."

"This doesn't involve lives," Mr. Swaine said. "It involves the

Chinese grabbing something that belongs to the United States. The normal thing to do in these cases is, you issue a démarche and demand it be returned ASAP."

Senator John McCain, Republican of Arizona, criticized the Obama administration for what he called a failure to provide a "strong and determined U.S. response" to Chinese actions in the South China Sea. "Freedom of the seas and the principles of the rules-based order are not self-enforcing," he said. "American leadership is required for their defense. But that leadership has been sorely lacking."

There was no immediate comment from Mr. Trump or his transition team.

EDWARD WONG contributed reporting.

China Agrees to Return Seized Drone, Ending Standoff, Pentagon Says

BY JANE PERLEZ AND MATTHEW ROSENBERG | DEC. 17, 2016

BEIJING — The Pentagon on Saturday said that Beijing had agreed to return an underwater drone seized by China in international waters, an indication that the two countries were moving to resolve an unusual incident that risked sharpening tensions in the run-up to the inauguration of President-elect Donald J. Trump.

"Through direct engagement with Chinese authorities, we have secured an understanding that the Chinese will return the U.U.V. to the United States," said Peter Cook, the Pentagon press secretary, using initials to refer to the Navy's unmanned underwater vehicle.

Mr. Cook said the deal had been reached after the United States "registered our objection to China's unlawful seizure of a U.S. unmanned underwater vehicle operating in international waters in the South China Sea."

The Chinese authorities told American officials that they planned to return the drone, but the two sides were still working out where, when and precisely how the device would be handed back, said two Defense Department officials, both of whom would talk about the negotiations with China only on the condition of anonymity. One of the officials said the Pentagon expected the matter to be resolved in the coming days without further acrimony.

The Pentagon statement came hours after China warned that the highly charged episode would not be resolved easily.

In a statement late Saturday, the Chinese Defense Ministry said it was in talks with the United States but criticized Washington for what it called an "inappropriate" exaggeration of the dispute. The American reaction, it said, is "not conducive to solving the problem smoothly."

"We hereby express regrets for that," it said.

Although the ministry said the drone would be returned to the United States in a "proper way," the statement stopped short of saying when or how the device, which Chinese and American analysts say was most likely used to gather intelligence about Chinese submarine activity in contested waters, would be returned, or if it would be handed back intact.

President-elect Donald J. Trump entered the fray Saturday morning, accusing China on Twitter of acting improperly. "China steals United States Navy research drone in international waters — rips it out of water and takes it to China in unprecedented act," he said.

The overseas edition of The People's Daily, the Communist Party's flagship newspaper, said on its social media account Saturday night that the Chinese capture of the drone was legal because rules about drone activities had not been clearly written. "This is the gray area," the newspaper said. "If the U.S. military can send the drone, surely China can seize it."

In its statement, the Defense Ministry scolded the United States over what it called its longstanding practice of conducting "close-in reconnaissance and military surveys" in waters claimed by China. The Chinese government has often complained to senior American officials, including President Obama, that the United States repeatedly intrudes by air and ship into waters close to China. The ministry's statement reiterated the complaint, saying "China firmly opposes it and urges the U.S. side to stop such operations."

A Chinese naval vessel seized the drone, which had been launched on Thursday from an American ship, the Bowditch, in waters off the Philippines. The American crew was in the process of retrieving the device when a small boat dispatched from the Chinese vessel took it as the American sailors looked on.

The action came two weeks after Mr. Trump angered Beijing by speaking by phone to the leader of Taiwan, and almost a week after he criticized China for building military bastions in the South China Sea. American officials were trying to determine whether the seizure was a response to Mr. Trump or whether it was just one more escalatory step in China's long-term plan to try to push the United States Navy out of the South China Sea, one of the world's busiest commercial and military waterways.

The Pentagon formally protested the capture of the drone, saying it was stolen American military property. The Pentagon said the drone had been carrying out scientific research, and asked China to return it. American experts, however, said the drone might have been designed to help follow China's submarine buildup, a critical part of the country's growing naval strength as it seeks unfettered control of the South China Sea and unimpeded access to the Pacific and Indian oceans.

A retired Chinese rear admiral, Yang Yi, speaking earlier at a conference sponsored by a state-run newspaper, The Global Times, said the Americans had invited the Chinese sailors to take the drone by sailing in the waters close to the Scarborough Shoal, fishing grounds that are claimed by China and the Philippines.

The Americans "deliver these things to our home," and it would be more than natural for Chinese sailors to seize the drone and examine it, Admiral Yang said.

"If Trump and the American government dare to take actions to challenge the bottom line of China's policy and core interests," he said, "we must drop any expectations about him and give him a bloody nose."

Reached by telephone, the president of a state-affiliated think tank, Wu Shicun, said the United States had most likely been conducting intelligence reconnaissance to detect Chinese submarine routes in the South China Sea. Mr. Wu, who heads the National Institute for South China Sea Studies and advises the government on maritime matters, described the drone "as a new way for the United States to conduct intelligence gathering."

"Previously the United States conducted surveillance with warships in the nearby waters of China, or by aircraft," he said. "Now the unmanned underwater vehicle is a new approach." The Chinese were justified in taking the unmanned underwater vehicle, he said.

The episode occurred in seas about 50 miles northwest of Subic Bay, a major port of the Philippines and a former United States Navy base, the Pentagon said. That means the Bowditch was within 200 miles of Scarborough Shoal, American analysts said.

The American vessel appeared to be outside the perimeter of the "nine-dash line," said Mira Rapp-Hooper, a senior fellow at the Center for a New American Security. China drew the line in the late 1940s as it laid claim to about 90 percent of the South China Sea.

"China has no legal basis to take actions like these on the high seas, but doing so outside Beijing's ambiguous claim line is particularly egregious and will make the incident especially hard to justify," Ms. Rapp-Hooper said.

The president of the Philippines, Rodrigo Duterte, who is nurturing warm ties with China and has warned he may break longstanding military relations with the United States, took a conciliatory approach over the Chinese action.

"I will not impose anything on China," he said at a news conference in Manila on Saturday. "Why? Because politics in Southeast Asia is changing." This was a reference to his tilt away from the United States, a treaty ally, since taking office in June. He referred to China as "the kindest soul of all."

The Philippines also took a forgiving attitude after the release of satellite images on Wednesday by the Center for Strategic and International Studies that appeared to show that China has installed weapons on the seven artificial islands it has built in the Spratly archipelago, not far from the Philippines in the South China Sea.

"There is nothing that we can do about that now, whether or not it is being done for purposes of further militarizing these facilities that they have put up," the foreign secretary, Perfecto Yasay Jr., said, reflecting the weak state of the Philippines military. "We cannot stop China at this point in time and say, 'Do not put that up.' "

By seizing the drone so close to the Philippines, China may have been trying to further weaken the already frayed United States alliance with Manila, American experts said.

The conciliatory reaction by the Philippines, even as the United States was making stern demands on Beijing, would complicate Washington's efforts to convince China that its actions were unacceptable, a senior American military official said on Saturday.

In an important ruling in July, an international tribunal in The Hague decided against China, saying that the Scarborough Shoal was entitled only to a 12-mile territorial zone, not 200 miles as the Chinese assert. China has refused to recognize the ruling.

Mr. Duterte on Saturday said he was ignoring the Hague ruling even though the case had been brought by the previous Philippines government. "In the play of politics now, I will set aside the arbitral ruling," he said.

The drone incident, according to a Pentagon account, began when a Chinese Navy vessel that was shadowing the Bowditch — a common practice in the South China Sea — pulled up not far from the ship. It then dispatched a small boat to seize the drone as the American crew was recovering it from the water. The Pentagon described the vehicle as an unclassified "ocean glider" system used to gather military oceanographic data such as salinity, water temperature and sound speed.

An American naval expert did not disagree with Mr. Wu's notion of what the Americans were probably doing. "Warfare and surveillance in the age of drones has not yet developed an agreed-upon set of rules," said Lyle J. Goldstein, an associate professor at the China Maritime Studies Institute at the United States Naval War College, in Rhode Island.

"This is increasingly a major problem as both China and the U.S. are deploying ever more air and naval drones into the contested waters and airspace of the Western Pacific," he said.

The seizure may have been just another way for Beijing to provoke the United States in a gray zone, just under the threshold of actual hostilities, Mr. Goldstein said. He said it was a time for "cooler heads to prevail," to halt a cycle of escalation that "cannot end well for either side."

In some respects, the seizure was not a surprise but just another step in China's increased harassment of the American Navy in the South China Sea, several American naval experts said.

In March 2009, soon after President Obama took office, five Chinese ships swarmed an American surveillance vessel, the Impeccable, 75 miles off Hainan island, the southernmost province of China. The Impeccable was towing sonar equipment designed for anti-submarine warfare, and the Chinese ships got as close as 25 feet from the ship in what the Pentagon called "illegal and dangerous" maneuvers.

JANE PERLEZ reported from Beijing, and MATTHEW ROSENBERG from Washington. FELIPE VILLAMOR contributed reporting from Manila. YUFAN HUANG contributed research.

Muted U.S. Response to China's Seizure of Drone Worries Asian Allies

BY JANE PERLEZ | DEC. 18, 2016

BEIJING — Only a day before a small Chinese boat sidled up to a United States Navy research vessel in waters off the Philippines and audaciously seized an underwater drone from American sailors, the commander of United States military operations in the region told an audience in Australia that America had a winning military formula.

"Capability times resolve times signaling equals deterrence," Adm. Harry B. Harris Jr. told a blue-chip crowd of diplomats and analysts at the prestigious Lowy Institute in Sydney, the leading city in America's closest ally in the region.

In the eyes of America's friends in Asia, the brazen maneuver to launch an operation against an American Navy vessel in international waters in the South China Sea about 50 miles from the Philippines, another close American ally, has raised questions about one of the admiral's crucial words. It was also seen by some as a taunt to President-elect Donald J. Trump, who has challenged the One China policy on Taiwan and has vowed to deal forcefully with Beijing in trade and other issues.

"The weak link is the resolve, and the Chinese are testing that, as well as baiting Trump," said Euan Graham, the director of international security at the Lowy Institute. "Capability, yes. Signaling, yes, with sending F-22 fighter jets to Australia. But the very muted response means the equation falls down on resolve."

Across Asia, diplomats and analysts said they were perplexed at the inability of the Obama administration to devise a strong response to China's challenge. It did not even dispatch an American destroyer to the spot near Subic Bay, a former American Navy base that is still frequented by American ships, some noted.

After discussions at the National Security Council on how to deal with the issue, the Obama administration demanded the return of the

President Obama at a news conference last week. Across Asia, diplomats and analysts said they were perplexed at the inability of the Obama administration to devise a strong response to China's seizing of an American underwater drone.

drone. On Saturday, China said it would comply with the request but did not indicate when or how the equipment would be sent back.

The end result, analysts said, is that China will be emboldened by having carried out an act that amounted to hybrid warfare, falling just short of provoking conflict, and suffering few noticeable consequences.

"Allies and observers will find it hard not to conclude this represents another diminishment of American authority in the region," said Douglas H. Paal, the vice president for studies at the Carnegie Endowment for International Peace.

Significantly, the Chinese grabbed the drone not only in international waters but outside even the "nine-dash line" that China uses as a marker for its claims in the South China Sea. In so doing, analysts said, Beijing was making the point that the entire sea was its preserve, even though it is entirely legal for the United States to conduct military operations in waters within 200 miles of the Philippines, an area known as an exclusive economic zone.

In the last dozen years, China has steadily showed off its growing military prowess to the countries around the South China Sea, which carries trillions of dollars of world trade and which China values for its strategic access to the Western Pacific and the Indian Ocean.

As China has built up its navy and its submarine fleet in the last decade, it has also emphasized what it calls its "inherent" right to dominate the regional seas, and to challenge the presence of the United States, its allies and partners in Asia.

The drone episode, which occurred on Thursday and was first broadcast by CNN despite efforts by the Obama administration to settle it quietly, was of a different nature and just as disquieting as past confrontations with China that involved bigger ships and more dangerous maneuvers, analysts said.

In 2001, soon after President George W. Bush came to office, an American spy aircraft, an EP-3, was forced to land on Hainan Island after colliding with a Chinese fighter jet. The Chinese stripped the plane of its assets and returned it broken down to its parts and packed in boxes.

In 2009, two months after President Obama took office, Chinese vessels swarmed a United States Navy reconnaissance ship, the Impeccable, in what the Pentagon said were dangerous and unprofessional maneuvers.

This time, China chose a more unconventional method to challenge the United States and hastened the timetable, challenging a president-elect rather than a newly installed president as it has in the past.

The drone itself, known as an unmanned underwater vehicle, was not a particularly important piece of equipment. Such drones are deployed to gather military oceanographic data and are available over the counter for about $150,000, the Pentagon said. Data from the drone would no doubt be used to help track China's growing submarine fleet, naval experts said.

More important than the equipment was the principle of freedom of navigation in international waters, and whether China was in the process of imposing its own rules in the South China Sea — more than 800 miles away from its coastline, said Alexander Vuving, a specialist on Vietnam at the Asia-Pacific Center for Security Studies in Hawaii.

"This is China showing that it is in the process of setting the rules in the South China Sea, imposing its own view in the South China Sea and saying the South China Sea should be its own backyard," Mr. Vuving said.

"If China can get away with this incident with impunity," he added, "this will send a chilling message to countries in the region."

Some leaders, like President Rodrigo Duterte of the Philippines, will feel validated in a pivot away from the United States toward China, Mr. Vuving said. "Others, like the Vietnamese, will have to seriously rethink their regional outlook."

Vietnam — always fearful of China, its neighbor to the north, but also careful not to alienate Beijing — has tried in the last few years to draw closer to the United States, while still maintaining a careful distance.

In 2011, as China became more assertive in the South China Sea, Vietnam accused China of instructing three high-speed patrol boats to cut the cables of a Vietnamese oil and gas survey ship.

The authoritarian Vietnamese government was so furious that it allowed anti-Chinese demonstrations in Hanoi.

In 2014, China moved a billion-dollar oil rig to waters close to the Paracel Islands that both Vietnam and China claim, and then blasted a flotilla of Vietnamese ships with water cannon.

Since then, China has hardened its position, sometimes referring to the South China Sea as a "core interest" in which there is no room for compromise, though others in the region call it bullying by the Chinese president, Xi Jinping.

Under that vision, China would be in control from the waters of Indonesia to Brunei, Malaysia, the Philippines and up to Japan.

In the East China Sea, China and Japan are at odds over an uninhabited island chain, known as the Senkaku in Japan and the Diaoyu in China. In June, China sent a warship for the first time into the waters around the islands, further escalating tensions.

Japan has been more outspoken than other Asian countries in its support for the Obama administration's objections to China's construction of military facilities on seven artificial islands in the South China Sea.

But in Tokyo, the government was watching the outcome of the drone episode with some anxiety. So far, Washington's restrained response has not been reassuring.

Obama Hoped to Transform the World. It Transformed Him.

OPINION | BY ADAM SHATZ | JAN. 12, 2017

WHEN BARACK OBAMA entered office, the hopes that he raised in his own country were exceeded only by the hopes he raised abroad. Mr. Obama tapped into those hopes with his inspirational rhetoric about a "transformational" presidency, and his promises were scarcely less dramatic. America would be steered back on track, working with other countries to meet the challenges of what he often called an "interdependent" world, from terrorism and poverty to financial crisis and global warming.

Rapturous crowds thrilled to his speech in Berlin in 2008, a few months before he was elected; less than a year into his presidency, the jury in Oslo awarded him a Nobel Peace Prize for his "vision" of a world without nuclear weapons, as if he were a poet rather than a head of state. Expectations ran so high that few spotted the contradictions in Mr. Obama's project, which sought to usher America into an era of relative decline and yet still somehow achieve transformative results. Being commander in chief prevented Mr. Obama from speaking frankly about the growing constraints on American power. But no one would experience them more sharply — or more frustratingly.

This was, in part, the legacy handed down to him by George W. Bush's truly transformational presidency, which envisioned a post-Cold War order of limitless American power. Mr. Bush created a new reality in the Middle East and trapped Mr. Obama in a war he had opposed in Iraq, and one that couldn't be won in Afghanistan. Though he sought to reduce America's footprint, Mr. Obama would distinguish himself as an even more zealous hunter of terrorists than Mr. Bush, presenting the assassination of Osama bin Laden as a centerpiece of his re-election campaign, even as he made no secret of seeing terrorism as an exaggerated threat. Extraordinary measures were required

The president's 2009 speech in Cairo, broadcast in a cafe in Baghdad.

to begin undoing the extraordinarily destructive Bush legacy, but Mr. Obama proved mostly incapable of them. He did not transform the world; the world transformed him.

Eight years ago, Mr. Obama suggested a messenger from a dreamy, multicultural future: the son of a Kenyan father and a white American mother; a well-traveled cosmopolitan who had spent much of his childhood in Indonesia, seemingly at home wherever he planted his feet. His vision of international diplomacy stressed the virtues of candid dialogue, mutual respect and bridge building. His famous address to the Islamic world, given at Cairo University in 2009, was a judicious balance sheet of past wrongs and an eloquent plea to turn a new page in history.

"Real power," the president told Jeffrey Goldberg of The Atlantic last year, "means you can get what you want without having to exert violence." Exhibit A, in the Obama years, was the Iran deal, which not only peacefully prevented Tehran from developing a nuclear weapon, but also brought about a thaw in Iran's relations with the West.

But that deal, along with a climate change agreement and a rapprochement with Cuba, was a rare success. The arc of recent history has not bent toward Mr. Obama's cosmopolitan vision of an interdependent world. On the contrary, the world — and America itself — is increasingly bedeviled by the tribalism that horrified him on a visit to his relatives in Kenya. In "Dreams From My Father," he writes of arriving with "simple formulas for Third World solidarity," only to discover that most Kenyans "worked with older maps of identity, more ancient loyalties," and that his liberal humanism fell on deaf ears.

Nowhere was such tribalism more incendiary than in the Middle East, thanks in large part to Mr. Obama's predecessor. Before the invasion of Iraq, Sunni and Shiite Muslims lived side by side, and often intermarried, under authoritarian states and a regional balance of power that provided stability, if not democracy. Mr. Bush put an end to that fragile balance. Iraq was liberated from Saddam Hussein, but the result was sectarian warfare, fueled by a struggle between Iran and Saudi Arabia.

The Arab Spring stirred hopes of reversing this bleak trend, and Mr. Obama initially gambled on its success, defying old allies like Saudi Arabia and Israel and expressing support for pro-democracy movements in Egypt and Tunisia. In these revolts, he saw an opportunity not only to improve America's image in the Middle East but also to end the Muslim world's isolation. From the ruins of the Arab revolts a new age would emerge, but its key players would be tribally minded strongmen and armed militants. And for aid and inspiration they would look not to the West but to the Persian Gulf states, Iran, Turkey and other regional power brokers.

Mr. Obama not only adapted to the shape of Middle Eastern power politics, but he also largely overlooked human rights abuses by Saudi Arabia, Israel, Egypt and other allies. The Bush administration's patronizing rhetoric of democracy promotion was shelved, but this came at the cost of reducing American concerns in the Middle East to terrorism and national security.

In a speech to the Turkish Parliament in 2009, Mr. Obama promised that "America's relationship with the Muslim community, the Muslim world cannot, and will not, just be based on opposition to terrorism." Yet that is precisely what happened, even if the "war on terror" was decorously renamed the "fight to counter violent extremism." The war was based on Special Operations and drone strikes rather than torture and ground invasions, but it, too, was subject to few restraints, and eventually it came to cover a much greater land mass. Styling himself as an anti-terrorist commander, Mr. Obama buried the legalistic multilateralism that he had taught at Harvard. While the drone program began under Mr. Bush, Mr. Obama substantially expanded it. Armed with a "kill list" and the Predator joystick, he could eliminate America's enemies, while avoiding land wars — or public scrutiny.

Mr. Bush's occupations provoked liberal outrage; Mr. Obama's drone war emitted a kind of white noise that most Americans ignored. But the killing of people by drones or Special Operations was not unnoticed in Yemen, Somalia and Pakistan or other countries, and did little to win local hearts and minds. In fact, his determination to avoid American casualties, even as he expanded the battlefield, reinforced the impression that for all his talk of cooperation and partnership, he was a pitiless realist.

That realism was at its most glacial in the case of Syria's civil war. Chastened by the results of NATO's intervention in Libya, where a dictator was replaced by militia rule and jihadist violence, and always a reluctant humanitarian, Mr. Obama understood that the Syrian war was as much a sequel to the bloody sectarian struggle inside Iraq as it was the latest installment of the Arab Spring. He drew a cold but defensible conclusion: The growth of the Islamic State was a direct threat to American interests that merited a military response, but President Bashar al-Assad was not. Intervention against Mr. Assad would lead to clashes with Russia, for whom Syria was a core interest.

At first glance, the twists and turns of Mr. Obama's Syria policy made the president seem indecisive, if not incoherent: calling for Mr.

Assad to step down without taking direct action against him, even after the regime's use of chemical weapons in defiance of Mr. Obama's "red line"; attacking the jihadists of the Islamic State while allies like Turkey and Qatar supported other extremist groups; opposing Russian designs and then coordinating airstrikes with Moscow. But the aim of keeping American troops out of Syria was consistent. At his final news conference as president, Mr. Obama expressed anguish over the fall of Aleppo, but insisted that his Syria policy had been guided by his sense of "what's the right thing to do for America."

It may well have been; American lives were spared. But noninterference created a vacuum that autocrats like President Vladimir V. Putin of Russia and Recep Tayyip Erdogan of Turkey were happy to fill. What's more, Mr. Obama's understanding of American interests in Syria was more restrictively drawn than one might have expected from a man so worldly, someone who had always stressed the interdependence of the global community and the moral burdens of "what it means to share this world in the 21st century." Who governs Syria may not be a core American interest, but the country's apocalyptic splintering is another matter. The effect of Mr. Obama's caution, as much as Moscow's belligerent resolve, was to help prolong the war.

The consequences of Syria's disintegration have spread far beyond its borders. Not only has the crisis placed dangerous strains on neighboring states, but it has emboldened the far right in Europe, which has played on fears about Islam and terrorism in its campaign against immigration and the European Union. Nor has the United States been unscathed by what Mr. Obama recently called the "tug of tribalism": Donald J. Trump owes his election to it. Mr. Trump is an open admirer of tribal politicians like Mr. Putin, Mr. Erdogan and Prime Minister Benjamin Netanyahu of Israel, not least because they remind him of himself with their love of the mob, contempt for liberal elites and penchant for conspiracy theory.

In his 2009 speech in Cairo, Mr. Obama imagined Muslim and Western democrats working together in partnership, overcoming borders imposed by war, prejudice and mistrust for the sake of a common future. Instead, the very prospect of a common future, of global interdependence, has been jeopardized by the emergence of an illiberal world of tribes without flags. Despite the best of intentions, and for all his fine words, Mr. Obama became one of the midwives of this dangerous and angry new world, where his enlightened cosmopolitanism increasingly looks like an anachronism.

ADAM SHATZ is a contributing editor at The London Review of Books and a fellow in residence at the New York Institute for the Humanities.

U.S. Removes Libya From List of Zones With Looser Rules for Drone Strikes

BY CHARLIE SAVAGE | JAN. 20, 2017

WASHINGTON — Before ceding power, the Obama administration quietly removed a former extremist stronghold in Libya from a list of combat zones where United States counterterrorism drone strikes are authorized without obeying special rules intended to prevent civilian deaths, officials said on Friday.

The change means that as Donald J. Trump's presidency begins, the United States is targeting Islamist militants in three known "areas of active hostilities," where strict guidelines to protect civilians do not apply: Afghanistan, Iraq and Syria. For much of 2016, there was a fourth: The region around Surt, Libya.

It is not clear whether Mr. Trump will keep those civilian-protection rules — called the "Presidential Policy Guidance," or P.P.G. — for airstrikes outside of active war zones. Issued by Mr. Obama in 2013, they require "near certainty" that a bombing will kill no civilians, and that the target must pose a threat to Americans — not just to American interests.

The Obama administration developed the guidelines in response to criticism that airstrikes were killing too many civilians, and in turn fueling anti-Americanism and helping terrorists recruit new members. But some military and C.I.A. officials have chafed under the limits.

Mr. Trump's team has not said what it will do with the 2013 rules. But a statement posted on the White House website after he was sworn in on Friday said the new administration would "pursue aggressive joint and coalition military operations when necessary" to defeat the Islamic State.

Last August, after the fledgling Libyan government asked for help in dislodging militants from the city of Surt, the Obama administration

Barack Obama and Donald J. Trump at the presidential swearing-in ceremony at the United States Capitol on Friday. It was not clear whether Mr. Trump would keep in place civilian-protection rules established by Mr. Obama in 2013.

quietly designated it an "area of active hostilities," where the guidelines to prevent civilian deaths did not apply. The change gave the military a freer hand to target Islamic State fighting positions and equipment. Under ordinary combat rules established by the laws of war, some bystander deaths are permissible if deemed necessary and proportionate.

At the time, the government did not announce that Mr. Obama had exempted Surt from the extra safeguards established by the 2013 rules. The New York Times first reported the change in late November.

Between August and December, the military said it carried out 435 airstrikes to drive out the Islamic State from Surt, a campaign called Operation Odyssey Lightning. It concluded the campaign on Dec. 19.

But Mr. Obama this week briefly turned Odyssey Lightning back on, and expanded its geographic scope, to authorize a major airstrike on Jan. 19 against suspected Islamic State training camps in the desert about 25 miles southwest of Surt. The bombings killed more than 80 militants, the military said. It did not report any civilian deaths, but said it was still evaluating the results.

In response to questions from The Times on Friday, officials at the Pentagon said that when Odyssey Lightning ended last month, so also did the military's authority to carry out airstrikes in Surt without obeying the 2013 rules. But when Mr. Obama briefly revived the operation for the strikes this week, its exemption from those rules was temporarily turned back on too, they said.

Col. Mark Cheadle, a spokesman for the United States Africa Command, said the expanded targeting authority expired again at midnight between Jan. 19 and Jan. 20, and now "there are no more" areas in Libya where the 2013 rules do not apply.

The administration had offered a clue that Surt was no longer exempted from the 2013 rules in a report the Office of the Director of National Intelligence issued late Thursday.

The report summarized official estimates of militants and civilians killed last year in counterterrorism airstrikes where the 2013 safeguards generally applied. But it also mentioned that areas of active hostilities, where the protections do not apply, currently include Afghanistan, Iraq, and Syria. It made no mention of Libya.

The report also said that in 2016, the United States carried out 53 such airstrikes that killed between 431 and 441 militants and one civilian. Those figures apparently include a huge airstrike in Somalia in March that killed about 150 people at what the military said was a graduation ceremony for Islamist fighters.

The government disclosed Thursday's report under an executive order Mr. Obama issued last July requiring annual public disclosure of casualty estimates from counterterrorism airstrikes away from active-hostilities zones. That order was part of a broader effort late in Mr. Obama's tenure to make the government less secretive about drone strikes. It is also not clear whether Mr. Trump will keep that requirement.

Preventing a Free-for-All With Drone Strikes

EDITORIAL | BY THE NEW YORK TIMES | MARCH 16, 2017

FOR NEARLY A DECADE, drone strikes have been central to America's counterterrorism policy. Operated from remote locations, the small aircraft can hover over targets for long periods of time and kill extremists with precision without risking American casualties. President Barack Obama found drones so effective and useful that over two terms, he approved 542 strikes that killed 3,797 people in non-battlefield areas where American forces were not directly engaged, including Pakistan, Yemen and Somalia.

But this seductive tool of modern warfare has a dark side. Seemingly bloodless and distant, drone strikes can tempt presidents and military commanders to inflict grave damage without sufficient forethought, violating sovereign rights and killing innocent civilians. Civilian deaths during Mr. Obama's tenure undermined American counterterrorism operations and became a recruiting tool for more extremists.

Mr. Obama was persuaded to impose sensible constraints on the use of drone strikes between 2013 and 2016. The White House would decide which individuals outside of the traditional war zones of Iraq and Afghanistan could be targeted, and there had to be "near certainty" that no civilians would be killed. In traditional war zones, military commanders make these decisions without interagency review, and the threshold for acceptable civilian casualties is less strict.

Now comes disturbing news: President Trump and his administration are moving to dilute or circumvent the Obama rules. This could have disastrous outcomes, not least because Mr. Trump seems even more enticed by drone warfare than Mr. Obama was. In the days since his inauguration, the tempo of airstrikes has increased significantly.

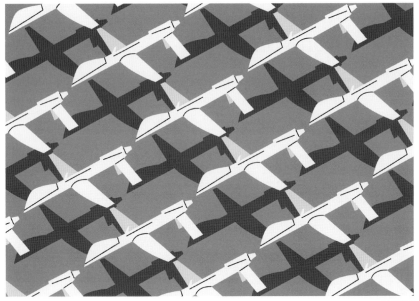

Mr. Trump has already granted a Pentagon request to declare parts of three provinces in Yemen, where Saudi Arabia is fighting Iranian-backed Houthis rebels, to be an "area of active hostilities." This, The Times has reported, would enable more permissive battlefield rules to apply. The president is also expected to soon approve a Pentagon proposal to do the same for parts of Somalia, where militants of the Shabab who are linked to Al Qaeda threaten regional stability. Both designations are supposed to be temporary, giving the administration time to decide whether to rescind or relax the Obama rules more broadly.

Military commanders often chafe at civilian oversight. But there is no evidence that the Obama rules have slowed counterterrorism efforts, and there are good reasons to keep them in place, including the fact that the legal basis for such strikes lacks credibility because Congress never updated the 2001 authorization for war in Afghanistan to take account of America's expanded military action against terrorists in Syria, Yemen and Libya.

Mr. Trump should heed the advice of national security experts who have urged the retention of strict standards for using force in non-battlefield areas and warned how even a small number of civilian deaths or injuries can "cause significant strategic setbacks" to American interests. He has already seen how a badly executed mission can have disastrous results: the raid in Yemen in January that resulted in the deaths of a member of the Navy's SEAL Team 6 and numerous civilians, including children.

And as most experts agree, killing terrorists does not by itself solve the threat from extremists. For that, Mr. Trump will need a comprehensive policy that also deals with improved governance in the countries where terrorists thrive and with ways to counter their violent messages on social media.

Trump Poised to Drop Some Limits on Drone Strikes and Commando Raids

BY CHARLIE SAVAGE AND ERIC SCHMITT | SEPT. 21, 2017

WASHINGTON — The Trump administration is preparing to dismantle key Obama-era limits on drone strikes and commando raids outside conventional battlefields, according to officials familiar with internal deliberations. The changes would lay the groundwork for possible counterterrorism missions in countries where Islamic militants are active but the United States has not previously tried to kill or capture them.

President Trump's top national security advisers have proposed relaxing two rules, the officials said. First, the targets of kill missions by the military and the C.I.A., now generally limited to high-level militants deemed to pose a "continuing and imminent threat" to Americans, would be expanded to include foot-soldier jihadists with no special skills or leadership roles. And second, proposed drone attacks and raids would no longer undergo high-level vetting.

But administration officials have also agreed that they should keep in place one important constraint for such attacks: a requirement of "near certainty" that no civilian bystanders will be killed.

The proposal to overhaul the rules has quietly taken shape over months of debate among administration officials and awaits Mr. Trump's expected signature. Despite the preservation of the protections for civilians, the other changes seemed likely to draw criticism from human rights groups.

The policy paves the way for broader and more frequent operations against Al Qaeda, the Islamic State and other jihadists. It would also apply in countries where the United States has targeted Islamist militants outside of regular combat for years, including Yemen, Somalia and Libya, and would ease the way to expanding such gray-zone acts of sporadic warfare to elsewhere in Africa, Asia and the Middle East where terrorists operate.

The policy, while containing significant changes, also preserves a key structure of President Barack Obama's approach to counterterrorism: dividing the world into war zones and places where higher protections for civilians apply. The elements of continuity suggest that as the war on terrorism drifts toward its 17th year, political, legal, diplomatic and practical hurdles constrain the Trump administration from making more radical policy shifts.

Last month, when he delivered a speech outlining his security policies for Afghanistan and the rest of South Asia, Mr. Trump vowed to loosen restrictions on hunting down terrorists.

"The killers need to know they have nowhere to hide, that no place is beyond the reach of American might and American arms," he said. "Retribution will be fast and powerful."

In May 2013, Mr. Obama imposed the rules on kill-or-capture operations by the military or the C.I.A. outside war theaters like Afghanistan, Iraq and Syria. The plan would extend Mr. Trump's pattern of giving broader day-to-day authority to the Pentagon and the C.I.A. — authorizing the agencies to decide when and how to conduct high-risk counterterrorism operations that Mr. Obama had insisted be used sparingly and only after top officials across the government reviewed them.

The move would also grant a C.I.A. push for permission to expand its program of covert drone strikes, which has included occasional attacks in Yemen and Syria but has largely centered on the tribal region of Pakistan, to Afghanistan — until now the exclusive purview of the military.

A cabinet-level committee of the top leaders of national-security agencies and departments approved the proposed new rules — called the P.S.P., for "Principles, Standards and Procedures" — at a meeting on Sept. 14 and sent the document to Mr. Trump, the officials said. They spoke on the condition of anonymity to describe sensitive discussions about a policy that is not yet final or public. A spokesman for the National Security Council did not contest their account but declined to comment.

One senior administration official described the proposed changes as primarily aimed at making much of the "bureaucracy" created by

Mr. Obama's 2013 rules, the Presidential Policy Guidance, or P.P.G., "disappear."

The official argued that the replacement rules should be seen as similar to Mr. Obama's but clearer and less bureaucratic — meaning drone operators and commanders would face fewer internal hurdles to launching specific strikes or raids.

By clearing the way to target rank-and-file Islamist insurgents even without the presence of a high-level leader focused on attacking Americans, the new approach would appear to remove some obstacles for possible strikes in countries where Qaeda- or Islamic State-linked militants are operating, from Nigeria to the Philippines.

However, the new plan would still require higher-level approval to start conducting strikes or raids in new countries under "country plans" that would be reviewed every 12 months. And under international law, the United States would probably also still need to obtain consent from a country's leaders to use force on their soil to strike at lower-level militants who pose no direct threat to the United States, weakening any self-defense argument.

Even before Mr. Obama left office, the evolving terrorism threat put pressure on the limits that were imposed in 2013. At the time, Al Qaeda was still reeling from the killing of Osama bin Laden, combat troops had left Iraq and were being reduced in Afghanistan, and operations outside war theaters seemed destined to be limited to occasional airstrikes aimed at individual "high-value targets" in Pakistan and Yemen, such as Qaeda leaders.

But the Islamic State has arisen and spread in the years since, and the military, especially while partnering with local governments, has found ways to get exceptions to Mr. Obama's rules — winning temporary exemptions to strike in various regions or justifying airstrikes on groups of lower-level militants as a matter of self-defense.

Several Obama administration counterterrorism officials had been bracing for a more complete dismantling of their handiwork, and they offered tentative praise for the prospect that their successors will keep in place heightened standards to protect civilians outside war zones. They had argued that avoiding bystander deaths was crucial not just for humanitarian reasons, but also to maintain support among allied governments and local populations and to keep from fueling terrorist propaganda and recruiting.

If the requirement of near certainty that no civilians be killed remains in place, "that's a real testament to the fact that it was not political or Obama being overly concerned about human rights; preventing civilian casualties is something our operators have seen as really important," said Luke Hartig, a senior director for counterterrorism at the National Security Council during the Obama administration.

It remains to be seen whether Mr. Trump will sign off on keeping the protections for civilians. During deliberations, some officials had argued for more leniency, but administration officials decided the risks outweighed the benefits.

International law governing war or self-defense allows countries to knowingly kill some civilians as an incidental consequence of attacking a legitimate military target, so long as the bystander deaths are deemed necessary and proportionate.

But some international law scholars, European allies and human rights groups disagree with the United States' position that war zone rules — like a right to attack militants based only on their status as enemy fighters, even if they do not pose a literally imminent threat at that moment — apply to counterterrorism strikes outside conventional battlefields.

Zeke Johnson, senior director of programs for Amnesty International USA, objected to the prospect of Mr. Trump eliminating the requirement that individual targets each pose a threat to Americans.

"The Obama administration's policy guidance on the use of lethal force was a positive step but fell far short on human rights protections," he said. "Any decision to weaken those standards would be a grave mistake."

The updated rules would continue to limit such strikes to members of groups that the executive branch has deemed to be covered by the aging congressional Authorization for Use of Military Force against the perpetrators of the Sept. 11 attacks, including Al Qaeda, the Islamic State and their associated forces.

Earlier this year, Mr. Trump agreed to a Pentagon request to exempt large swaths of Yemen and Somalia from the 2013 rules by declaring them to be "areas of active hostilities," temporarily bringing them under less restrictive war-zone rules. However, the head of the military's Africa Command, Gen. Thomas D. Waldhauser, decided on his own to keep the targeting limit of near-certainty that no civilians would die for strikes in Somalia.

U.S. Drone Strike Kills Militants in Pakistan but Angers Its Government

BY SALMAN MASOOD | JAN. 24, 2018

ISLAMABAD, PAKISTAN — A leader of the militant Haqqani network and two of his aides were killed Wednesday in an American drone strike in northwestern Pakistan, an attack that was denounced by the Pakistani government.

The attack took place on Wednesday morning in the Speen Thal Dapa Mamozai area of the Kurram tribal region and was directed at a house that the Pakistani authorities said was being used by Afghan refugees. The militant commander, Nasir Mehmood, who was also known as Khawari, and two of his aides were killed.

The Haqqani network, affiliated with the Taliban and designated as a terrorist group by the United States, has carried out numerous deadly attacks in Afghanistan in recent years. The presence of its leaders and militants in Pakistan and its links with the country's military intelligence agency have long caused friction between the United States and Pakistan.

The Kurram region has been used frequently by Haqqani network fighters to cross into neighboring Afghanistan.

American officials have repeatedly demanded that the Pakistanis take action against the Haqqani network, but Pakistani officials deny that the militants have any organized presence inside the country.

Wednesday's attack was at least the third American drone strike in the past two months in Pakistani territory.

Pakistan's Ministry of Foreign Affairs condemned Wednesday's drone strike as a violation of the country's sovereignty.

"Pakistan has continued to emphasize to the U.S. the importance of sharing actionable intelligence so that appropriate action is taken against terrorists by our forces within our territory," the ministry said in a statement. "Such unilateral actions, as that of today, are detrimental to the spirit of cooperation between the two countries in the fight against terrorism."

Pakistani military and civil officials insisted that Wednesday's attack struck an Afghan refugee camp, which they said validated their stance that Afghan refugees be sent back to Afghanistan.

At least 2.7 million Afghan refugees are living in various parts of the country, and Pakistani military officials say the refugee camps and settlements provide shelter to Taliban and Haqqani militants.

"There are no organized militant sanctuaries inside Pakistan any-more," said Maj. Gen. Asif Ghafoor, a Pakistani military spokesman. "Afghan refugees, including 1.2 million unregistered, are difficult to trace. The militants morph into refugees. This is the reason we feel repatriation of Afghan refugees is essential."

U.S. and Pakistan Give Conflicting Accounts of Drone Strike

BY SALMAN MASOOD | JAN. 25, 2018

ISLAMABAD, PAKISTAN — One day after an American drone strike killed a leader of the militant Haqqani network in northwestern Pakistan, United States officials on Thursday rejected a claim by Pakistan that the strike had targeted an Afghan refugee camp.

There were also conflicting accounts of the location of the drone strike and the number of people killed.

A statement by Pakistan's Ministry of Foreign Affairs on Wednesday condemned the strike and maintained that it had "targeted an Afghan refugee camp in Kurram Agency" — an assertion that the United States rejected on Thursday.

"The claim in an M.F.A. statement yesterday that U.S. forces struck an Afghan refugee camp in Kurram Agency yesterday is false," said Richard W. Snelsire, the United States Embassy spokesman in Islamabad, Pakistan's capital.

American officials said that there were no Afghan refugee camps in Kurram, a remote tribal region straddling the border with Afghanistan, where they said Wednesday's drone strike had taken place. The strike, which killed Nasir Mehmood, a commander of the Taliban-affiliated Haqqani network, was at least the third American drone strike in the past two months in Pakistani territory.

The United Nations refugee agency also said it had not been operating in the tribal regions of Pakistan since 2005. "We don't have any access to FATA," Qaisar Khan Afridi, the agency's spokesman said, referring to the semiautonomous tribal regions.

But Pakistani officials maintain that there are 43 Afghan refugee settlements in Khyber-Pakhtunkhwa Province, and that some of the settlements overlap with the adjoining tribal regions.

The Pakistani military said in a statement that the drone strike had singled out a house in one such settlement in the province's Hangu District, and that Afghan refugees were present in the settlement. The settlement was not an "organized terrorist sanctuary," it said.

A Pakistani security official, speaking on the condition of anonymity as he was not authorized to speak to the news media, said that the confusion about the location had arisen as the targeted house was in a settlement at the junction of the Kurram, North Waziristan and Hangu regions.

The number of people killed in the strike was also disputed. Although initial reports from the remote region said that two of the commander's aides had died in the strike, the local news media reported on Thursday that only two people in total had been killed. The Pakistani security official said the security forces could confirm only the militant commander's death.

The conflicting accounts of the drone strike are yet another strain in an already difficult relationship between the United States and Pakistan. This month the Trump administration announced that it would suspend nearly all security aid to Pakistan, an across-the-board freeze reflecting Washington's frustration with what it considers to be a refusal by the country to crack down on terrorist networks operating there.

The Haqqani network has carried out numerous high-profile deadly attacks in Afghanistan in recent years.

The presence of its leaders and militants in Pakistan and its links with the country's military intelligence agency have long soured relations between the United States and Pakistan.

IHSANULLAH TIPU MEHSUD contributed reporting.

Learning From Israel's Political Assassination Program

REVIEW | BY KENNETH M. POLLACK | MARCH 7, 2018

RISE AND KILL FIRST
The Secret History of Israel's Targeted Assassinations
By Ronen Bergman
Translated by Ronnie Hope
Illustrated. 753 pp. Random House. $35

ONE OF THE very first things I was taught when I joined the C.I.A. was that we do not conduct assassinations. It was drilled into new recruits over and over again.

Today, it seems that all that is left of this policy is a euphemism.

We don't call them assassinations anymore. Now, they are "targeted killings," most often performed by drone strike, and they have become America's go-to weapon in the war on terror.

There have been many who have objected, claiming that the killings inspire more attacks on the United States, complicate our diplomacy and undermine our moral authority in the world. Yet the targeted killings drone on with no end in sight. Just counting the campaigns in Pakistan, Yemen and Somalia, the Bush administration conducted at least 47 targeted killings by drones, while under the Obama administration that number rose to 542.

America's difficult relationship with targeted killing and the dilemmas we may face in the future are beautifully illuminated by the longer story of Israel's experiences with assassination in its own endless war against terrorism. Israel has always been just a bit farther down this slippery slope than the United States. If we're willing, we can learn where the bumps are along the way by watching the Israelis careening ahead of us.

Americans now have a terrific new introduction to that story with the publication of Ronen Bergman's "Rise and Kill First: The Secret History of Israel's Targeted Assassinations." It's easy to understand why Bergman's book is already a best seller. It moves at a torrid pace and tells stories that would make Jason Bourne sit up and say "Wow!" It is smart, thoughtful and balanced, and the English translation is superb. It deserves all of the plaudits it has already received.

A word of warning: Bergman is properly focused on the narrow story of Israel's targeted killings. Other aspects of its lifelong counterterrorism struggle are largely absent. For instance, Israel's "security barriers" against the West Bank and Gaza, highly controversial and highly successful, are not even mentioned. For those looking for a more comprehensive account, try Daniel Byman's outstanding "A High Price: The Triumphs and Failures of Israeli Counterterrorism," or Ami Pedahzur's older but still insightful "The Israeli Secret Services and the Struggle Against Terrorism."

Yet the biggest thing (almost) left out of Bergman's book is that targeted killing offers no end to the terrorism. Targeted killings are a tactic, not a strategy. Only at the very end of "Rise and Kill First" is this problem confronted, and only because Bergman himself puts it squarely on the table before finishing his narrative. That's a compliment, not a criticism of Bergman, because it reflects the inability of Israel's own national security community to solve this problem, and too often even to acknowledge it.

What Bergman demonstrates is that targeted killing can be a highly effective tactic to neutralize terrorist cells and can be part of a powerful operational approach to cripple terror groups. Israel's internal security agency, known as Shin Bet, believes that every successful killing of a suicide bomber saves 16 to 20 Israeli lives.

But it does not offer a strategic answer to the problem of terrorism because it cannot defeat the broader movements that breed and feed the terrorist groups. Like some modern-day hydra, no matter how many heads Israel chops off, the beast always grows new ones — sometimes more dangerous than before.

Terrorism is a form of insurgency, and the way that nations have learned to defeat it is by applying what we now call counterinsurgency (COIN) strategy. The core of a COIN strategy is to suppress the groups' military operations while addressing the underlying grievances that inspire the movement behind them. It is ultimately what is meant by the worn phrase "winning hearts and minds."

Israel has a big problem here. Targeted killings, barriers and other security activities can suppress terror attacks, but it is not at all clear that Israel can ever win the hearts and minds of the Palestinians, the crucial foundation for Palestinian terrorist groups. It had the same problem with the Shiites of Lebanon and their support for Hezbollah. That's because the Israeli occupation is a central grievance of the Palestinians, as it was for Lebanon's Shiites.

Israeli military officers have devoured the vast literature on COIN warfare, eagerly adapting its tactics and operational methods. However, ask an Israeli soldier or general about the strategic aspects of COIN and they almost invariably insist that it's wrong. They will claim that they tried to win hearts and minds in Gaza and the West Bank and it just didn't work because it just doesn't work.

Only a few will acknowledge that the problem is not with COIN strategy, but with Israel's ability to execute the strategy without doing something that is politically … hard. The deepest truth is that Israel so far has not tried the one thing that could address the underlying grievances that give life to its terrorist enemies, trading land for peace. Some of Israel's brightest counterterror minds know this. It is why the senior leadership of its defense and intelligence establishments are typically so committed to the peace process, as revealed by the 2012 Israeli documentary "The Gatekeepers."

Today many Israelis are justifiably skeptical that they have a partner for peace. Many Palestinians are justifiably skeptical that Israel is a partner for peace.

Regardless of whether you believe one side, the other, or both, it still means that the most obvious approach Israel might try to find a strategic end to the problem of terrorism is off the table. Israel's political right has insisted that there are one-state solutions that could address Palestinian grievances, but the plans they have presented so far seem fanciful, and the Israeli government has shown no inclination to try them.

Some in the current Israeli government seem to believe that its new covert alliances with Sunni Arab states like Saudi Arabia and the United Arab Emirates against Iran will furnish a strategic path out — that the Arab states will persuade the Palestinians to give up and reconcile themselves to Israeli suzerainty. One can't be certain it won't work, but you shouldn't bet money that it will.

Since Israel cannot or will not employ the core strategic approach of COIN, it is left with nothing but tactics, targeted killings high among them. It consigns Israel to endless repression, endless assassinations, endless criticism and endless racking internal debate like that which Bergman diligently recounts.

All of this holds inevitable lessons for the United States. The most successful counterterror campaigns in American history rested on strategic efforts to undermine the popular movements behind the terrorist groups. In 2006-8, in Iraq, George W. Bush's surge strategy crippled the Sunni Arab terrorist groups by helping Sunni Arabs defend themselves, granting them economic benefits and political power, and shutting down the ethnic cleansing campaigns of the Shiite militias. It was a virtuoso effort that eliminated the grievances of the Sunni community, at least until the United States and Nuri al-Maliki let them come roaring back after 2010.

Yet when it comes to fighting terrorism in places like Pakistan, Yemen, Somalia, Niger and Libya, the tactics — starting with targeted killing by drone — are all we seem willing to employ. It consigns us to the same kind of endless war that the Israelis seem ready to bear. Yet how sure are we that America's people and political system are as inured to the forever war as Israel's claim to be?

By the end of Bergman's book, targeted killing feels almost like a drug that Israel uses to treat the worst symptom (terrorism) of a terrible disease (Palestinian anger). It is a very effective drug, but it treats only the symptom and so offers no cure. It is also a very addictive one, in part because it is so effective at suppressing the symptoms.

I fear that we are all becoming targeted-killing junkies, unable to kick the habit and unwilling to treat the disease that got us hooked in the first place.

KENNETH M. POLLACK is a resident scholar of the American Enterprise Institute.

CHAPTER 5

Scrutiny Falls on the Pentagon's Shadow War and Drone Business

Increased airstrikes in Libya raised questions regarding drone policy and operations in northern Africa, particularly about the Pentagon's possible expansion of its "shadow war" against terrorists in African nations. Plans to initiate armed drone missions from Niger drew further commentary from critics and diplomats. As the counterterrorism campaign expanded in northwestern Africa, President Trump sought to expand the business of armed drone sales. Efforts to improve drone artificial intelligence entered the news cycle as well: The Pentagon sought to maintain and extend Google's involvement in the pilot program Project Maven, which drew protest from Google employees.

Under Trump, U.S. Launched 8 Airstrikes Against ISIS in Libya. It Disclosed 4.

BY ERIC SCHMITT | MARCH 8, 2018

WASHINGTON — The United States military has carried out twice as many airstrikes against Islamic State militants in Libya since President Trump took office as it has publicly acknowledged, raising questions about whether the Pentagon has sought to obscure operations in the strife-torn North African nation.

The total number of strikes — eight since January 2017 — is relatively small. But the uptick points to the threat that the Trump administration believes Libya still poses, despite the president's focus on the American-led campaign against the Islamic State in Syria and Iraq that he has trumpeted as one of his administration's signature national security accomplishments.

Counterterrorism specialists warn that the Islamic State and Al Qaeda also still pose formidable threats in places like Somalia, Yemen and West Africa. On Tuesday, Gen. Thomas D. Waldhauser, the head of the Africa Command, said in congressional testimony that "we are heavily involved in the counterterrorism piece" in Libya.

On its website and in news releases, the Africa Command has acknowledged only four airstrikes in Libya in the last 14 months against the Islamic State, also called ISIS, ISIL or Daesh. All of the attacks have been carried out since September.

But on Thursday, a spokesman for the command, Maj. Karl J. Wiest, said four other previously undisclosed airstrikes had been carried out against Islamic State militants, most recently in January.

Commanders decided to reveal those strikes only if a reporter specifically asked about them, a practice the Pentagon calls "responses to questions," Major Wiest said via telephone and email from the Africa Command's headquarters in Stuttgart, Germany. He said journalists, usually tipped off by local reporting in Libya, have called about some but not all of the four strikes.

Major Wiest said the additional four strikes were not disclosed when they happened to protect American-backed forces or diplomatic issues. "We're not trying to hide anything," he said. "Our goal is always to be as transparent as possible while taking into account operational security, force protection and diplomatic sensitivities."

He could not explain why the command did not announce the strikes some days later, after the sensitivities were presumably resolved or otherwise went away. Of the previously undisclosed airstrikes, one was launched in September, two in October and one in January.

The Defense Department "doesn't want to telegraph its moves, nor discuss the outcome of surgical strikes because it wants to keep the enemy scared and guessing," Rudolph Atallah, a former director of African counterterrorism policy for the Pentagon, said in an email from Tunis. "There is regional cooperation to make sure Daesh doesn't continue to expand its footprint because many of its core members are originally North African."

Bill Roggio, editor of the Foundation for Defense of Democracies' Long War Journal, which tracks military strikes against militant groups, said the Africa Command was "transparent when asked, but perhaps not always forthcoming when it comes to issuing statements or updating its website."

To be sure, the number of American airstrikes in Libya since Mr. Trump took office — carried out largely by armed MQ-9 Reaper drones flying from an air base in Sicily — is tiny in comparison to the number of strikes carried out against militants in Yemen (more than 130) or Somalia (more than 40) in the same period.

And it pales in comparison to airstrikes against the Islamic State in Iraq and Syria, where the American-led coalition has bombed on a near-daily basis.

The United States has only a few dozen Special Operations forces on the ground in Libya, advising and assisting militias aligned with the country's fragile Government of National Accord, which clings perilously to power in the capital, Tripoli.

Only a handful of countries, including China and Turkey, operate embassies in Tripoli with full-time staffs. The United States Embassy has temporarily relocated to Tunis.

Critics say the Trump administration has yet to arrive at a coherent policy for Libya. On one hand, the president has said he sees no role for the United States in Libya; on the other, he has said the United States must fight the Islamic State there.

Nonetheless, the airstrikes are significant because they are a kind of barometer of the highly volatile political and security environment in the country. They also serve as an indicator of the vast ungoverned spaces that still offer fertile safe havens where Islamic State and Qaeda fighters can regroup.

"ISIS-Libya remains a formidable regional terrorist threat," Lt. Gen. Robert Ashley, the head of the Defense Intelligence Agency, told the Senate Armed Services Committee in written testimony this week. "Al Qaeda affiliates in Libya are spreading their influence, particularly in the ungoverned southern region."

A United Nations report, issued on Feb. 12, offered a similarly gloomy assessment.

"While no longer in control of territory, ISIL continues to be active in Libya and retains the ability to conduct complex terrorist attacks," the report noted. It also described "desert units" operating in south and central Libya, and "sleeper cells" that lie in wait elsewhere in the country.

The additional strikes came to light during testimony that General Waldhauser gave to the House Armed Services Committee. In response to a question, the general said there had been eight strikes against the Islamic State in Libya in the past year — twice the number his command had publicly acknowledged.

In September, the Pentagon persuaded Mr. Trump to approve a limited action against the Islamic State in Libya. American drones struck a training camp there on Sept. 22, killing 17 militants. The militants were shuttling fighters in and out of the country and stockpiling weapons, the command said.

Four days later, another round of American airstrikes rained down 100 miles southeast of Surt, killing several more fighters, the Pentagon said. The command quickly announced those attacks.

But it did not announce a strike on Sept. 29 that killed a small number of Islamic State fighters, about 100 miles southwest of Surt. Or on Oct. 9, when an airstrike killed another small group of militants, this time 250 miles south of Surt. Or on Oct. 18, when an attack killed another small group of fighters in Libya's Wasdi al Shatii. Or on Jan. 23, when two vehicles were destroyed in strikes near Fuqaha in central Libya.

The command did announce right away two other strikes, on Nov. 17 and Nov. 19, both near Fuqaha.

Just days before Mr. Trump took office, a B-2 bomber attack on an Islamic State training camp killed more than 80 militants, according to the Pentagon. In 2016, the military conducted nearly 500 airstrikes in Surt over several months to destroy the Islamic State stronghold.

U.S. Strikes Qaeda Target in Southern Libya, Expanding Shadow War There

BY DECLAN WALSH AND ERIC SCHMITT | MARCH 25, 2018

BENGHAZI, LIBYA — The United States military carried out its first ever drone strike against Qaeda militants in southern Libya this weekend, signaling a possibly significant expansion of the American counterterrorism campaign in the North African nation.

Until now, the Pentagon had focused its counterterrorism strikes in Libya almost exclusively on Islamic State fighters and operatives farther north — eight since President Trump took office. In 2016, the military conducted nearly 500 airstrikes in the coastal city of Surt over several months to destroy the Islamic State's stronghold there.

But the attack on Saturday that the military's Africa Command said had killed two militants — later identified by a spokeswoman as belonging to Al Qaeda's branch in northwestern Africa — took place in the country's southwest, a notorious haven for a deadly mix of Al Qaeda and other extremist groups that also operate in the Sahel region of Niger, Chad, Mali and Algeria.

"This appears to be the continuation of expanding AFRICOM activity in Libya's ungoverned areas," said Deborah K. Jones, who served as United States ambassador to Libya from 2013 to 2015, referring to the Africa Command.

A missile fired by the American drone struck a house in Ubari, 435 miles south of Tripoli, in an area close to major oil fields that was wracked by violent ethnic feuding in 2015. Pictures in Libyan news media outlets showed a mutilated corpse lying in the rubble of a house, and a pair of shrapnel-ridden vehicles nearby. Local residents were quoted by the media outlets as saying the house had been frequented by foreigners.

In a statement, the military's Africa Command said the strike had targeted militants with Al Qaeda in the Islamic Maghreb, an affiliate also known as AQIM, and had been carried out in coordination with the United Nations-backed unity government in Tripoli. "At this time, we assess no civilians were killed in this strike," the statement said.

The strike came as the Trump administration has been reassessing the American military commitment in North and West Africa after the ambush in Niger last fall that killed four American soldiers. The Pentagon has been preparing to fly armed drone missions from Niger's capital, Niamey, a step that diplomats and analysts say could further widen the Pentagon's shadow war in this part of the continent.

In a sign of how the Pentagon has sought to obscure its operations in Libya and other parts of northwestern Africa, the Africa Command did not announce the strike on Saturday.

It responded to questions from The New York Times late Saturday with a terse statement after media reports about the strike circulated in Libya. The statement did not identify where the drone had originated.

Earlier this month, in response to a Times query, the Pentagon acknowledged for the first time that Green Berets working with government forces in Niger had killed 11 Islamic State fighters in a firefight in December. No Americans were hurt in that fight, the Pentagon said. Ubari is at the intersection of the powerful criminal and jihadist currents that have washed across Libya in recent years. Roughly equidistant from Libya's borders with Niger, Chad and Algeria, the area's seminomadic tribesmen are heavily involved in the smuggling of weapons, drugs and illegal migrants through the lawless deserts of southern Libya.

Some have allied with Islamist militias, including Al Qaeda in the Islamic Maghreb, which operates across Algeria, Mali, Niger and Libya.

The area erupted into conflict in 2014 when a century-old peace treaty between the Tuareg and Tebu ethnic groups collapsed over a dispute about control of the fuel smuggling trade. The fighting, which occurred independently of the broader struggle for control of Libya after the 2011 overthrow of Col. Muammar el-Qaddafi, raged for a year, killing hundreds and leaving many families displaced.

The Tebu and Tuareg eventually struck a peace agreement, and a neutral militia currently keeps the peace in Ubari, but tensions remain. In November, Turkish engineers working at the city power station were kidnapped by unidentified gunmen, as was a Pakistani engineer at the station who went missing this month, according to local news media reports.

While some Tebu groups have allied with the United Nations-backed government in Tripoli, Tuareg factions have allied with Qaeda, which is also believed to have profited from the trade in smuggled fuel.

In the statement on Saturday, Robyn M. Mack, a spokeswoman for the United States Africa Command, said that it was still assessing the results of the strike and that the purpose had been "to deny terrorists freedom of action and degrade their ability to reconsolidate."

But the command did not answer several other questions: Who were the two dead militants, and why were they important enough to kill with an airstrike? What role, if any, did France play in a region of Libya in which it has also conducted counterterrorism operations? And, most significantly, to what extent is the attack the start of an escalating campaign against a broad spectrum of extremists in northwestern Africa, or a one-off strike against high-profile Qaeda operatives?

"Beginning a concerted strike campaign against AQIM or other AQ elements in the Sahel, akin to what we are doing in Yemen and Somalia, would mark a significant expansion of our counterterrorism efforts," said Luke Hartig, a former senior director for counterterrorism at the National Security Council during the Obama administration.

"If this is going to be the start of a broader campaign, it would be helpful to hear more from the administration about the threat posed by AQIM and why it merits putting our people in harm's way and conducting strikes," Mr. Hartig said.

A senior French security official said France had played no role in the strike, but added that Paris was "very happy of this continued commitment of the U.S. to counterterrorism in Libya."

Questions about whether the American military, under the Trump administration, is seeking to blur the expanding scope of operations in Africa were raised this month when it was revealed that the United States had carried out four airstrikes in Libya between September and January that Africa Command did not disclose at the time. The military has said it will acknowledge such missions if asked about them, even if it does not affirmatively disclose them in a news release.

Ms. Mack said that Saturday's attack was the first airstrike the United States had conducted against Al Qaeda in Libya. In fact, the United States conducted an airstrike in eastern Libya in June 2015 against Mokhtar Belmokhtar, the mastermind of the 2013 terrorist seizure of an Algerian gas plant that left 38 foreign hostages dead. Mr. Belmokhtar was a longtime Qaeda operative with ties to senior Qaeda leadership in Pakistan. Western intelligence officials today remain divided over whether he is dead.

American efforts to hunt down Islamists in Libya's vast deserts rely heavily on surveillance and airpower but also on alliances with the armed groups vying for control of Libya. Mohamed El Sallak, a spokesman for the United Nations-backed unity government, said on Twitter that the attack in Ubari on Saturday was part of the "strategic cooperation between Libya and the United States in the fight against terrorism."

But in Ubari, armed Tebu and Tuareg groups have sided with different sides in Libya's chaotic struggle, and the unity government is by no means the dominant player.

Some control a stretch of southern border, while others have allied with militias from the coastal cities of Misurata and Benghazi. The rising force now in the south is Field Marshal Khalifa Hifter, the commander of the Libyan National Army based in Benghazi.

Since his forces ousted the last Islamist militias from Benghazi in December, Mr. Hifter has focused on the south, where he exerts influence through his fleet of aging warplanes and alliances with local armed groups.

In Sebha, the largest southern city, Mr. Hifter and the rival United Nations-backed government are vying for control through local proxies. In Ubari, 110 miles to the west, Mr. Hifter has allied with an ethnically mixed militia that is composed of former Qaddafi loyalists and more recent recruits.

DECLAN WALSH reported from Benghazi, and **ERIC SCHMITT** from Washington. **SULIMAN ALI ZWAY** contributed reporting from Berlin.

American Drone Strike in Libya Kills Top Qaeda Recruiter

BY ERIC SCHMITT | MARCH 28, 2018

AN AMERICAN MILITARY DRONE strike over the weekend in southern Libya killed a top recruiter and logistics specialist for Al Qaeda's branch in northwest Africa, the Pentagon said on Wednesday, and a senior military official warned of more attacks on extremists there.

The military's Africa Command said in a statement that the attack killed two militants, one of whom was identified as Musa Abu Dawud, a high-ranking official in Al Qaeda in the Islamic Maghreb, known as AQIM.

Mr. Dawud trained Qaeda recruits in Libya for strike operations in the region, and provided logistics, money and weapons that enabled the group to threaten and attack American and Western interests, the military statement said.

Until now, the Pentagon had focused its counterterrorism strikes in Libya — eight since President Trump took office — almost exclusively on Islamic State fighters and operatives farther north. Over several months in 2016, the military conducted nearly 500 airstrikes in the coastal city of Surt to destroy the Islamic State's stronghold there.

The missile fired by the American drone on Saturday was the first in southern Libya. It struck a house in Ubari, 435 miles south of Tripoli, in the country's southwest, a notorious haven for a deadly mix of Al Qaeda and other extremist groups that also operate in the Sahel region of Niger, Chad, Mali and Algeria.

The area is also close to major oil fields that were crippled by violent ethnic feuding in 2015.

"I wouldn't say this is the beginning of a wider campaign," Col. Mark Cheadle, the Africa Command's chief spokesman, said in an email. But, he added, "If we find targets we can strike, and it is appropriate to do so, I think we would certainly consider the option."

Colonel Cheadle said that Mr. Dawud was "a significant 'fixer' for Al Qaeda." Other American military officials said that Mr. Dawud had been under surveillance for a significant period of time but gave no details about how he was tracked to a house and killed with another Qaeda fighter. The command said that no civilians were believed to have been killed in the attack.

The State Department said in 2016 that Mr. Dawud was a "specially designated global terrorist." He began engaging in terrorist activity as early as 1992, the State Department said at the time.

Pictures in Libyan news outlets showed a mutilated corpse lying in the rubble of a house and a pair of shrapnel-ridden vehicles nearby. Residents were quoted as saying that the house had been frequented by foreigners.

The strike came as the Trump administration has been reassessing the American military commitment in North and West Africa after an ambush in Niger in October that killed four American soldiers. The Pentagon has been preparing to fly armed drone missions from Niger's capital, Niamey, a step that diplomats and analysts say could further widen the Pentagon's shadow war in that part of the continent.

The American military is also building a $100 million drone base in Agadez, north of Niamey, that is set to begin operations this year.

In a sign of how the Pentagon has sought to obscure its operations in Libya and other parts of northwestern Africa, the Africa Command initially did not announce the strike. It responded to questions from The New York Times late Saturday with a terse statement after news reports about the strike circulated in Libya.

The command on Wednesday identified Mr. Dawud as the target of the attack and confirmed his death after "operational reporting" and an analysis of the strike's damage was complete. Questions about whether the American military, under the Trump administration, is blurring the scope of operations in Africa were raised this month when it was revealed that the U.S. had carried out four airstrikes in Libya from September to January that the Africa Command did not disclose at the time.

The command's statement, coupled with Colonel Cheadle's comments, left little doubt that American airstrikes could soon expand in southern Libya.

"Al Qaeda and other terrorist groups, such as ISIS, have taken advantage of undergoverned spaces in Libya to establish sanctuaries for plotting, inspiring and directing terror attacks," the statement said. "Left unaddressed, these organizations could continue to inflict casualties on the civilian populations and security forces, and plot attacks against U.S. citizens and allied interests in the region."

A Shadowy War's Newest Front: A Drone Base Rising From Saharan Dust

BY ERIC SCHMITT | APRIL 22, 2018

AIR BASE 201, NIGER — Rising from a barren stretch of African scrubland, a half-finished drone base represents the newest front line in America's global shadow war.

At its center, hundreds of Air Force personnel are feverishly working to complete a $110 Million airfield that, when finished in the coming months, will be used to stalk or strike extremists deep into West and North Africa, a region where most Americans have no idea the country is fighting.

Near the nascent runway, Army Green Berets are training Nigerien forces to carry out counterterrorism raids or fend off an enemy ambush — like the one that killed four American soldiers near the Mali border last fall.

Taken together, these parallel missions reflect a largely undeclared American military buildup outside the battlefields of Iraq and Afghanistan, often with murky authorities and little public attention, unfolding in remote places like Yemen, Somalia and, increasingly, West Africa.

In Niger alone, the Pentagon in the past few years has doubled the number of United States troops, to about 800 — not to conduct unilateral combat missions, but to battle an increasingly dangerous Al Qaeda, the Islamic State and even loosely associated extremist groups with proxy forces and drone strikes. The military's missions in Niger are expected to come under scrutiny in a long-awaited Defense Department investigation into the deadly Oct. 4 ambush that is nearing release.

"The base, and the more frequent flights that its opening will allow, will give us far more situational awareness and intelligence on a region that has been a hub of illicit and extremist activity," said P.W. Singer, a strategist at New America in Washington who has written extensively

An American Special Forces soldier training Nigerien troops during an exercise on the Air Base 201 compound.

about drones. "But it will also further involve us in yet more operations and fights that few Americans are even aware our military is in."

Questions about whether the American military, under the Trump administration, is seeking to obscure the expanding scope of operations in Africa surfaced last month when it was revealed that the United States had carried out four airstrikes in Libya between September and January that the military's Africa Command had failed to disclose at the time.

Soon after, the military acknowledged for the first time that Green Berets working with Nigerien forces had killed 11 Islamic State militants in a multiday firefight in December. No American or Nigerien forces were harmed in the December gun battle.

But the combat — along with at least 10 other previously unreported attacks on American troops in West Africa between 2015 and 2017 — underscored the fact that the deadly ambush in Niger was not an isolated episode. Nigerien forces and their American advisers are preparing other major operations to clear out militants, military officials say.

"It's essential that the American public is aware of, engaged in, and decides whether or not to support American military operations in countries around the world, including Niger," said Senator Chris Coons, Democrat of Delaware, who visited Niger with four other senators this month.

Six months after the fatal attack, which took place outside the village of Tongo Tongo near the Mali border, the Trump administration stands at a critical crossroad in the military's global counterterrorism campaign.

One path would push ahead with President Trump's campaign vow to defeat the Islamic State and other violent extremist organizations, not just in Iraq and Syria, but worldwide. The other would be to pull out and leave more of the fighting to allies, as Mr. Trump said he wants to do in Syria, possibly ceding hard-fought ground to militants.

During a counterterrorism exercise this past week in north-central Niger that drew nearly 2,000 military personnel from 20 African and Western countries, many officers voiced concerns that America's commitment in West Africa could fall victim to the latter impulse.

"It's important to still have support from the U.S. to help train my men, to help with our shortfalls," said Col. Maj. Moussa Salaou Barmou, commander of Niger's 2,000 Special Operations forces, who trained at Fort Benning, Ga., and the National Defense University in Washington.

In an interview on the sidelines of the exercise, Maj. Gen. J. Marcus Hicks, the head of American Special Operations forces in Africa, put it this way: "This is an insurance policy that's very inexpensive, and I think we need to keep paying into it."

Building a new base in this remote, landlocked country nearly twice the size of Texas marks the latest chapter in the military's contentious history of drone operations around the world.

An American airman near an overturned plane at the Agadez airfield.

It comes as American drone strikes are on the rise again, after tapering off somewhat in places like Pakistan. The number of American strikes against Islamist militants last year tripled in Yemen and doubled in Somalia from the figure a year before.

Last month, an armed drone flown from a second base in Niger killed a Qaeda leader in southern Libya for the first time, signaling a possible expansion of strikes there.

Where American and Nigerien officials see enhanced security in drone operations — for surveillance, strikes or protecting Special Forces patrols — others fear a potentially destabilizing impact that could hand valuable recruiting propaganda to an array of groups aligned with Al Qaeda and the Islamic State, and that could increase the militants' menace.

"Eliminating jihadi military leaders through drone operations could temporarily disorganize insurgent groups," said Jean-Hervé Jezequel, deputy director of the International Crisis Group's West Africa project

Construction of a hangar on the new American drone base last week in Agadez, Niger.

in Dakar, Senegal. "But eventually the void could also lead to the rise of new and younger leaders who are likely to engage into more violent and spectacular operations to assert their leadership."

A rare visit this month to Air Base 201, the largest construction project that Air Force engineers have ever undertaken alone, revealed several challenges.

Commanders grapple with swirling dust storms, scorching temperatures and lengthy spare-part deliveries to fix broken equipment. All have conspired to put the project more than a year behind schedule and $22 million over its original budget.

American officials have sought to allay fears of local residents that the base, just two miles outside the city of Agadez, could be a target for terrorist attacks — not a guardian against them. Rumors circulated that the dozens of dump trucks rumbling in and out of the heavily defended front gates each day were secretly stealing valuable uranium, for which the region is renowned.

TARA TODRAS-WHITEHILL FOR THE NEW YORK TIMES

Outside the Agadez mosque. American officials have sought to allay fears of local residents that the new drone base, just two miles outside Agadez, could be a target for terrorist attacks.

"We had to overcome some suspicion and distrust," said Lt. Col. Brad Harbaugh, commander of the 724th Expeditionary Air Base Squadron, the senior officer here.

For centuries, Agadez has been an important way-stop for smugglers, migrants and camel caravans traversing the Sahara. The city of 125,000 people is more than 450 miles from Tongo Tongo, where the American soldiers and Nigerien troops were attacked last fall, but militants have also targeted this region in recent years.

In May 2013, Islamist militants staged coordinated attacks, using suicide car bombs to strike a Nigerien military compound in Agadez and a French-operated uranium company in the nearby town of Arlit. Two groups claimed credit for the bombings, which Nigerien authorities said killed at least 24 soldiers and one civilian, as well as 11 militants.

President Barack Obama ordered the first 100 American troops to Niger in February 2013 to help set up unarmed surveillance drone operations in Niamey, Niger's capital, to support a French-led operation combating Qaeda and affiliated fighters in neighboring Mali.

Even as those troops deployed, military officials said then that they ultimately wanted to move the drone operations to outside Agadez, closer to Saharan smuggling routes that Islamist militants use to transport arms and fighters from Libya to northern Mali. Runway construction broke ground in the summer of 2016.

Niger's government approved Air Base 201 in 2014. Last November, a month after the deadly ambush, the government of Niger gave the Defense Department permission to fly armed drones out of Niamey, a major expansion of the American military's firepower in Africa. American and Nigerien officers here refused to discuss armed operations. But a Defense Department official acknowledged that the military in January started flying armed missions from Niamey, 500 miles southwest of the base, including the deadly strike in southern Libya last month.

MQ-9 Reaper drones, made by General Atomics, will be moved to Air Base 201 once its runway and hangars are completed by early next year, as will several hundred American troops. Roughly half of the 800 American forces in Niger — the second-largest American troop presence in Africa, second only to the 4,000 military personnel at a permanent base in Djibouti — work here now.

Bill Roggio, editor of the Long War Journal, a website run by the Foundation for Defense of Democracies that tracks military strikes against militant groups, said that moving the drone operations to Agadez had two main advantages.

First, he said, the base will be more centrally located to conduct operations throughout the Sahel, a vast area on the southern flank of the Sahara that stretches from Senegal to Sudan and has been seized by a growing wave of terrorism and armed conflict.

Second, Agadez is more isolated than Niamey. That will help keep the operations more low-key and away from prying eyes.

"The Agadez base has the potential to become the most active counterterrorism hub in Africa," Mr. Roggio said.

The Niger deployment is only the second time that armed drones have been stationed and used in Africa.

Drones now based in Djibouti are used in Yemen and Somalia, where there were about 30 strikes last year against Shabab and Islamic State targets — twice the number in 2016. Drones used against targets in Libya have flown from Sicily, but with a range of about 1,100 miles, the Reapers could not reach militant hide-outs in southern Libya.

The United States also flies unarmed surveillance drones from bases in Tunisia and Cameroon.

At Air Base 201, building a runway more than 6,800 feet long and 150 feet wide poses severe logistical hurdles. Rock from local quarries is crushed into gravel for the runway's underlying support. But the rock crushers have broken down, forcing workers at least once to use couriers to hand-deliver spare parts from Paris to avoid weekslong shipping delays.

"There's no Home Depot downtown here," said Colonel Harbaugh, 40, an Afghanistan war veteran from Pittsburgh.

Runway construction also requires choreographed precision.

Dump trucks disgorge piles of wet gravel. A giant grader equipped with a GPS-controlled blade spreads the rock to an exact depth. Steamrollers pace back and forth behind the grader to compact the gravel. To settle properly, the moistened rocks must not dry too quickly, so much of this work is done at night to avoid daytime temperatures that this past week soared to 107 degrees.

Later this summer, workers will lay five inches of asphalt atop the rock bed. In all, commanders say they will pave some 39 acres of airfield. While built mainly for the Reaper drones, the runway and adjoining taxiways and ramps must be able to handle much heavier C-17 cargo planes. Three huge hangars capped in a tan fabric covering sprout like giant mushrooms, visible from miles away. Each can fit one or more drones.

Eventually, the plan is to turn Air Base 201 completely over to the Nigerien military. American and Nigerien security forces now jointly patrol the 2,200-acre site. The base cafeteria employs 80 local workers, and the Americans have spent tens of millions of dollars on local rock, concrete, steel, wood and other supplies. Civic leaders and local journalists were recently invited to tour the base.

A four-man civil affairs team led by Capt. Andrew Dacey, a former Army infantry platoon leader in Iraq, has worked closely with civic, religious and educational leaders in Agadez to help address the high unemployment and ill-equipped schools — shortcomings that Islamist extremists can exploit.

The team is helping local schools start a metal and wood craftsman apprenticeship that teaches teenage students new skills and supplies classrooms with refurbished desks.

"The base has been very helpful for our security and our economy," said Mahaman Ali, an inspector for primary schools in the area, pointing to piles of broken desks that will be repaired.

TARA TODRAS-WHITEHILL FOR THE NEW YORK TIMES

Children attending classes at a makeshift tent school on the outskirts of Agadez. The Air Force donated supplies to the school, and is working on outreach programs within the community.

And yet doubts still linger about the base's enduring legacy.

"The deployment of armed drones is not going to make a strategic difference," said E.J. Hogendoorn, the International Crisis Group's deputy Africa program director in Washington, "and may even increase local hostility to the U.S. and the central government in distant Niamey."

HELENE COOPER and **THOMAS GIBBONS-NEFF** contributed reporting from Washington.

Trump Administration Seeks to Expand Sales of Armed Drones

BY GARDINER HARRIS | APRIL 19, 2018

WASHINGTON — A day after President Trump promised to slash the red tape involved in weapons sales, the administration announced on Thursday a new policy that could vastly expand sales of armed drones, a contentious emblem of the shift toward remotely controlled warfare.

That change, in addition to a newly released update to the policy governing which nations are allowed to buy sophisticated American-made weapons, is intended to accelerate arms sales, a key priority of Mr. Trump.

The president seemed to foreshadow the new policies on Wednesday night, when he said at a news conference with Prime Minister Shinzo Abe of Japan that after allies order weapons from the United States, "we will get it taken care of, and they will get their equipment rapidly."

"It would be, in some cases, years before orders would take place because of bureaucracy with Department of Defense, State Department," Mr. Trump said. "We are short-circuiting that. It's now going to be a matter of days. If they're our allies, we are going to help them get this very important, great military equipment."

The new policies, though, will do little to change the often yearslong intervals between orders and deliveries of weapons, but the State Department announced that it intended over the next 90 days to re-evaluate the process that can sometimes lead to such gaps.

Delays in delivering weapons systems have long been an irritant to foreign governments and domestic manufacturers, and almost every administration in the modern era has tried to fix the process. Top aides in the Trump White House have frequently called officials at the State Department and the Pentagon to try to hurry things along.

But the deals can pose an array of challenges, involving not only national security issues, such as the transfer of sensitive technologies, but also economic ones. India, the world's largest weapons buyer, often requires defense firms to build weapons in India in partnership with Indian firms, the kind of requirements that the Trump administration finds objectionable in China with regard to cars and other products.

The biggest change announced on Thursday involves the sale of larger armed drones like the Predator and the Reaper, which have been the workhorses of the fight against insurgents in Afghanistan and the tribal regions of Pakistan. President Barack Obama embraced the weapons but was also so troubled by such remote warfare tools that he placed unusual restrictions on their sale.

Those restrictions have allowed drone makers in Israel, China and Turkey to capture a large part of a market that American manufacturers had pioneered, something the Trump administration wants to reverse.

The new drone export policy "will level the playing field by enabling U.S. firms to increase their direct sales to authorized allies and partners," Peter Navarro, assistant to the president for trade and manufacturing policy, said in a news briefing on Thursday. He added, "This will keep our defense industrial base in the vanguard of emerging defense technologies while creating thousands of additional jobs with good wages and generating substantial export revenues."

Mr. Navarro noted that at last year's Paris Air Show, Chengdu Aircraft Industry Group of China showed off its Wing Loong II, a medium-altitude long-endurance drone that he described as a knockoff of General Atomics' Reaper. He said the market for such aircraft was expected to be $50 billion annually within a decade.

Under the old policy, only Britain, France and Italy were approved to purchase armed drones, according to Dan Gettinger, co-director of the Center for the Study of the Drone at Bard College.

As more countries are approved, "the risk is that countries may be more willing to use military force when they can do so without risking their own people," Mr. Gettinger said.

Sales of smaller, unarmed drones have fewer restrictions, and American manufacturers dominate the market for those, Mr. Gettinger said.

The newly announced changes in the policy governing which countries can purchase sophisticated American-made weapons, known as the Conventional Arms Transfer Policy, instruct the government to take domestic economic concerns into greater account than it has in the past.

The new policy also says that consideration should be given to minimizing civilian casualties. That could potentially justify sales of "smart" bombs, which are easier to direct to specific targets.

But experts said that the changes are not likely to have much effect on sales.

"I think it's political posturing," said Rachel Stohl, managing director of the Stimson Center, a think tank focusing on foreign policy. "We already sell to almost everybody in the world. Are we really going to open markets to places like Iran and North Korea now? I don't think so."

Human rights advocates denounced the changes as loosening rules they viewed as already too permissive. John Sifton, an advocacy director at Human Rights Watch, said that some of the changes were intended to make questionable arms sales easier to conduct.

"It's going to be easier to give licenses in cases like Saudi Arabia, which has a history of launching military strikes that harm huge numbers of civilians," Mr. Sifton said.

The Obama administration was also enthusiastic about foreign weapons sales, which soared during its tenure. Direct weapons sales declined in the first year of the Trump administration from the year before and are now roughly half the level seen in 2011, the first full year of the Arab Spring.

The policy changes were announced two days after a hearing on Capitol Hill during which senators from both parties expressed anguish at the vast humanitarian crisis in Yemen, caused in part by Saudi Arabia's use of American weapons.

"Maybe part of the humanitarian answer is supplying less weapons to a war," Senator Rand Paul, Republican of Kentucky, said during the hearing.

A bipartisan group of senators has proposed legislation that would require the State Department to routinely certify that Saudi Arabia is taking steps to end the suffering there, the sort of review that slows weapons purchases. The Trump administration opposes the legislation.

'The Business of War': Google Employees Protest Work for the Pentagon

BY SCOTT SHANE AND DAISUKE WAKABAYASHI | APRIL 4, 2018

WASHINGTON — Thousands of Google employees, including dozens of senior engineers, have signed a letter protesting the company's involvement in a Pentagon program that uses artificial intelligence to interpret video imagery and could be used to improve the targeting of drone strikes.

The letter, which is circulating inside Google and has garnered more than 3,100 signatures, reflects a culture clash between Silicon Valley and the federal government that is likely to intensify as cutting-edge artificial intelligence is increasingly employed for military purposes.

"We believe that Google should not be in the business of war," says the letter, addressed to Sundar Pichai, the company's chief executive. It asks that Google pull out of Project Maven, a Pentagon pilot program, and announce a policy that it will not "ever build warfare technology."

That kind of idealistic stance, while certainly not shared by all Google employees, comes naturally to a company whose motto is "Don't be evil," a phrase invoked in the protest letter. But it is distinctly foreign to Washington's massive defense industry and certainly to the Pentagon, where the defense secretary, Jim Mattis, has often said a central goal is to increase the "lethality" of the United States military.

From its early days, Google has encouraged employees to speak out on issues involving the company. It provides internal message boards and social networks where workers challenge management and one another about the company's products and policies. Recently, the heated debate around Google's efforts to create a more diverse work force spilled out into the open.

Google employees have circulated protest petitions on a range of issues, including Google Plus, the company's lagging competitor to Facebook, and Google's sponsorship of the Conservative Political Action Conference.

Employees raised questions about Google's involvement in Project Maven at a recent companywide meeting. At the time, Diane Greene, who leads Google's cloud infrastructure business, defended the deal and sought to reassure concerned employees. A company spokesman said most of the signatures on the protest letter had been collected before the company had an opportunity to explain the situation.

The company subsequently described its work on Project Maven as "non-offensive" in nature, though the Pentagon's video analysis is routinely used in counterinsurgency and counterterrorism operations, and Defense Department publications make clear that the project supports those operations. Both Google and the Pentagon said the company's products would not create an autonomous weapons system that could fire without a human operator, a much-debated possibility using artificial intelligence.

But improved analysis of drone video could be used to pick out human targets for strikes, while also better identifying civilians to reduce the accidental killing of innocent people.

Without referring directly to the letter to Mr. Pichai, Google said in a statement on Tuesday that "any military use of machine learning naturally raises valid concerns." It added, "We're actively engaged across the company in a comprehensive discussion of this important topic." The company called such exchanges "hugely important and beneficial," though several Google employees familiar with the letter would speak of it only on the condition of anonymity, saying they were concerned about retaliation.

The statement said the company's part of Project Maven was "specifically scoped to be for non-offensive purposes," though officials declined to make available the relevant contract language. The Defense Department said that because Google is a subcontractor on

Project Maven to the prime contractor, ECS Federal, it could not provide either the amount or the language of Google's contract. ECS Federal did not respond to inquiries.

Google said the Pentagon was using "open-source object recognition software available to any Google Cloud customer" and based on unclassified data. "The technology is used to flag images for human review and is intended to save lives and save people from having to do highly tedious work," the company said.

Some of Google's top executives have significant Pentagon connections. Eric Schmidt, former executive chairman of Google and still a member of the executive board of Alphabet, Google's parent company, serves on a Pentagon advisory body, the Defense Innovation Board, as does a Google vice president, Milo Medin.

In an interview in November, Mr. Schmidt acknowledged "a general concern in the tech community of somehow the military-industrial complex using their stuff to kill people incorrectly, if you will." He said he served on the board in part "to at least allow for communications to occur" and suggested that the military would "use this technology to help keep the country safe."

An uneasiness about military contracts among a small fraction of Google's more than 70,000 employees may not pose a major obstacle to the company's growth. But in the rarefied area of artificial intelligence research, Google is engaged in intense competition with other tech companies for the most talented people, so recruiters could be hampered if some candidates are put off by Google's defense connections.

As Google defends its contracts from internal dissent, its competitors have not been shy about publicizing their own work on defense projects. Amazon touts its image recognition work with the Department of Defense, and Microsoft has promoted the fact that its cloud technology won a contract to handle classified information for every branch of the military and defense agencies.

The current dispute, first reported by Gizmodo, is focused on Project Maven, which began last year as a pilot program to find ways to speed up the military application of the latest A.I. technology. It is expected to cost less than $70 million in its first year, according to a Pentagon spokeswoman. But the signers of the letter at Google clearly hope to discourage the company from entering into far larger Pentagon contracts as the defense applications of artificial intelligence grow.

Google is widely expected to compete with other tech giants, including Amazon and Microsoft, for a multiyear, multibillion-dollar contract to provide cloud services to the Defense Department. John Gibson, the department's chief management officer, said last month that the Joint Enterprise Defense Infrastructure Cloud procurement program was in part designed to "increase lethality and readiness," underscoring the difficulty of separating software, cloud and related services from the actual business of war.

The employees' protest letter to Mr. Pichai, which has been circulated on an internal communications system for several weeks, argues that embracing military work could backfire by alienating customers and potential recruits.

"This plan will irreparably damage Google's brand and its ability to compete for talent," the letter says. "Amid growing fears of biased and weaponized AI, Google is already struggling to keep the public's trust." It suggests that Google risks being viewed as joining the ranks of big defense contractors like Raytheon, General Dynamics and the big-data firm Palantir.

"The argument that other firms, like Microsoft and Amazon, are also participating doesn't make this any less risky for Google," the letter says. "Google's unique history, its motto Don't Be Evil, and its direct reach into the lives of billions of users set it apart."

Like other onetime upstarts turned powerful Silicon Valley behemoths, Google is being forced to confront the idealism that guided the company in its early years. Facebook started with the lofty mission of connecting people all over the world, but it has recently come under fire for becoming a conduit for fake news and being used by Russia to influence the 2016 election and sow dissent among American voters.

Paul Scharre, a former Pentagon official and author of "Army of None," a forthcoming book on the use of artificial intelligence to build autonomous weapons, said the clash inside Google was inevitable, given the company's history and the booming demand for A.I. in the military.

"There's a strong libertarian ethos among tech folks, and a wariness about the government's use of technology," said Mr. Scharre, a senior fellow at the Center for a New American Security in Washington. "Now A.I. is suddenly and quite quickly moving out of the research lab and into real life."

SCOTT SHANE reported from Washington, and DAISUKE WAKABAYASHI from San Francisco. CECILIA KANG contributed reporting from Washington.

How a Pentagon Contract
Became an Identity Crisis for Google

BY SCOTT SHANE, CADE METZ AND DAISUKE WAKABAYASHI | MAY 30, 2018

WASHINGTON — Fei-Fei Li is among the brightest stars in the burgeoning field of artificial intelligence, somehow managing to hold down two demanding jobs simultaneously: head of Stanford University's A.I. lab and chief scientist for A.I. at Google Cloud, one of the search giant's most promising enterprises.

Yet last September, when nervous company officials discussed how to speak publicly about Google's first major A.I. contract with the Pentagon, Dr. Li strongly advised shunning those two potent letters.

"Avoid at ALL COSTS any mention or implication of AI," she wrote in an email to colleagues reviewed by The New York Times. "Weaponized AI is probably one of the most sensitized topics of AI — if not THE most. This is red meat to the media to find all ways to damage Google."

Dr. Li's concern about the implications of military contracts for Google has proved prescient. The company's relationship with the Defense Department since it won a share of the contract for the Maven program, which uses artificial intelligence to interpret video images and could be used to improve the targeting of drone strikes, has touched off an existential crisis, according to emails and documents reviewed by The Times as well as interviews with about a dozen current and former Google employees.

It has fractured Google's work force, fueled heated staff meetings and internal exchanges, and prompted some employees to resign. The dispute has caused grief for some senior Google officials, including Dr. Li, as they try to straddle the gap between scientists with deep moral objections and salespeople salivating over defense contracts.

The advertising model behind Google's spectacular growth has provoked criticism that it invades web users' privacy and supports dubious websites, including those peddling false news. Now the company's path to future growth, via cloud-computing services, has divided the company over its stand on weaponry. To proceed with big defense contracts could drive away brainy experts in artificial intelligence; to reject such work would deprive it of a potentially huge business.

The internal debate over Maven, viewed by both supporters and opponents as opening the door to much bigger defense contracts, generated a petition signed by about 4,000 employees who demanded "a clear policy stating that neither Google nor its contractors will ever build warfare technology."

Executives at DeepMind, an A.I. pioneer based in London that Google acquired in 2014, have said they are completely opposed to military and surveillance work, and employees at the lab have protested the contract. The acquisition agreement between the two companies said DeepMind technology would never be used for military or surveillance purposes.

About a dozen Google employees have resigned over the issue, which was first reported by Gizmodo. One departing engineer petitioned to rename a conference room after Clara Immerwahr, a German chemist who killed herself in 1915 after protesting the use of science in warfare. And "Do the Right Thing" stickers have appeared in Google's New York City offices, according to company emails viewed by The Times.

Those emails and other internal documents, shared by an employee who opposes Pentagon contracts, show that at least some Google executives anticipated the dissent and negative publicity. But other employees, noting that rivals like Microsoft and Amazon were enthusiastically pursuing lucrative Pentagon work, concluded that such projects were crucial to the company's growth and nothing to be ashamed of.

Many tech companies have sought military business without roiling their work forces. But Google's roots and self-image are different.

"We have kind of a mantra of 'don't be evil,' which is to do the best things that we know how for our users, for our customers and for everyone," Larry Page told Peter Jennings in 2004, when ABC News named Mr. Page and his Google co-founder, Sergey Brin, "People of the Year."

The clash inside Google was sparked by the possibility that the Maven work might be used for lethal drone targeting. And the discussion is made more urgent by the fact that artificial intelligence, one of Google's strengths, is expected to play an increasingly central role in warfare.

Jim Mattis, the defense secretary, made a much-publicized visit to Google in August — shortly after stopping in at Amazon — and called for closer cooperation with tech companies.

"I see many of the greatest advances out here on the West Coast in private industry," he said.

Dr. Li's comments were part of an email exchange started by Scott Frohman, Google's head of defense and intelligence sales. Under the header "Communications/PR Request — URGENT," Mr. Frohman noted that the Maven contract award was imminent and asked for direction on the "burning question" of how to present it to the public.

A number of colleagues weighed in, but generally they deferred to Dr. Li, who was born in China, immigrated to New Jersey with her parents as a 16-year-old who spoke no English and has climbed to the top of the tech world.

Dr. Li said in the email that the final decision would be made by her boss, Diane Greene, the chief executive of Google Cloud. But Dr. Li thought the company should publicize its share of the Maven contract as "a big win for GCP," Google Cloud Platform.

She also advised being "super careful" in framing the project, noting that she had been speaking publicly on the theme of "Humanistic A.I.," a topic she would address in a March op-ed for The Times.

"I don't know what would happen if the media starts picking up a theme that Google is secretly building AI weapons or AI technologies to enable weapons for the Defense industry," she wrote in the email.

Asked about her September email, Dr. Li issued a statement: "I believe in human-centered AI to benefit people in positive and benevolent ways. It is deeply against my principles to work on any project that I think is to weaponize AI."

As it turned out, the company did not publicize Maven. The company's work as a subcontractor came to public attention only when employees opposed to it began protesting on Google's robust internal communications platforms.

The company promised employees that it would produce a set of principles to guide its choices in the ethical minefield of defense and intelligence contracting. Google told The Times on Tuesday that the new artificial intelligence principles under development precluded the use of A.I. in weaponry. But it was unclear how such a prohibition would be applied in practice.

At a companywide meeting last Thursday, Sundar Pichai, the chief executive, said Google wanted to come up with guidelines that "stood the test of time," employees said. Employees say they expect the principles to be announced inside Google in the next few weeks.

The polarized debate about Google and the military may leave out some nuances. Better analysis of drone imagery could reduce civilian casualties by improving operators' ability to find and recognize terrorists. The Defense Department will hardly abandon its advance into artificial intelligence if Google bows out. And military experts say China and other developed countries are already investing heavily in A.I. for defense.

But skilled technologists who chose Google for its embrace of benign and altruistic goals are appalled that their employer could eventually be associated with more efficient ways to kill.

Google's unusual culture is reflected in its company message boards and internal social media platforms, which encourage employees to speak out on everything from Google's cafeteria food to its diversity initiatives. But even within this free-expression workplace, longtime employees said, the Maven project has roiled Google beyond anything in recent memory.

When news of the deal leaked out internally, Ms. Greene spoke at the weekly companywide T.G.I.F. meeting. She explained that the system was not for lethal purposes and that it was a relatively small deal worth "only" $9 million, according to two people familiar with the meeting.

That did little to tamp down the anger, and Google, according to the invitation email, decided to hold a discussion on April 11 representing a "spectrum of viewpoints" involving Ms. Greene; Meredith Whittaker, a Google A.I. researcher who is a leader in the anti-Maven movement; and Vint Cerf, a Google vice president who is considered one of the fathers of the internet for his pioneering technology work at the Defense Department.

Because there was so much interest, the group debated the topic three times over one day for Google employees watching on video in different regions around the world.

According to employees who watched the discussion, Ms. Greene held firm that Maven was not using A.I. for offensive purposes, while Ms. Whittaker argued that it was hard to draw a line on how the technology would be used.

Last Thursday, Mr. Brin, the company's co-founder, responded to a question at a companywide meeting about Google's work on Maven. According to two Google employees, Mr. Brin said he understood the controversy and had discussed the matter extensively with Mr. Page and Mr. Pichai. However, he said he thought that it was better for peace if the world's militaries were intertwined with international organizations like Google rather than working solely with nationalistic defense contractors.

Google and its parent company, Alphabet, employ many of the world's top artificial intelligence researchers. Some researchers work inside an A.I. lab called Google Brain in Mountain View, Calif., and others are spread across separate groups, including the cloud computing business overseen by Ms. Greene, who is also an Alphabet board member.

Many of these researchers have recently arrived from the world of academia, and some retain professorships. They include Geoff Hinton, a Briton who helps oversee the Brain lab in Toronto and has been open about his reluctance to work for the United States government. In the late 1980s, Mr. Hinton left the United States for Canada in part because he was reluctant to take funding from the Department of Defense.

Jeff Dean, one of Google's longest-serving and most revered employees, who now oversees all A.I. work at the company, said at a conference for developers this month that he had signed a letter opposing the use of so-called machine learning for autonomous weapons, which would identify targets and fire without a human pulling the trigger.

DeepMind, the London A.I. lab, is widely considered to be the most important collection of A.I. talent in the world. It now operates as a separate Alphabet company, though the lines between Google and DeepMind are blurred.

DeepMind's founders have long warned about the dangers of A.I. systems. At least one of the lab's founders, Mustafa Suleyman, has been involved in policy discussions involving Project Maven with the Google leadership, including Mr. Pichai, according to a person familiar with the discussions.

Certainly, any chance that Google could move quietly into defense work with no public attention is gone. Nor has Dr. Li's hope to keep A.I. out of the debate proved realistic.

"We can steer the conversation about cloud," Aileen Black, a Google executive in Washington, cautioned Dr. Li in the September exchange, "but this is an AI specific award." She added, "I think we need to get ahead of this before it gets framed for us."

SCOTT SHANE reported from Washington, CADE METZ from London, and DAISUKE WAKABAYASHI from San Francisco.

Google Will Not Renew Pentagon Contract That Upset Employees

BY DAISUKE WAKABAYASHI AND SCOTT SHANE | JUNE 1, 2018

SAN FRANCISCO — Google, hoping to head off a rebellion by employees upset that the technology they were working on could be used for lethal purposes, will not renew a contract with the Pentagon for artificial intelligence work when a current deal expires next year.

Diane Greene, who is the head of the Google Cloud business that won a contract with the Pentagon's Project Maven, said during a weekly meeting with employees on Friday that the company was backing away from its A.I. work with the military, according to a person familiar with the discussion but not permitted to speak publicly about it.

Google's work with the Defense Department on the Maven program, which uses artificial intelligence to interpret video images and could be used to improve the targeting of drone strikes, roiled the internet giant's work force. Many of the company's top A.I. researchers, in particular, worried that the contract was the first step toward using the nascent technology in advanced weapons.

But it is not unusual for Silicon Valley's big companies to have deep military ties. And the internal dissent over Maven stands in contrast to Google's biggest competitors for selling cloud-computing services — Amazon.com and Microsoft — which have aggressively pursued Pentagon contracts without pushback from their employees.

Google's self-image is different — it once had a motto of "don't be evil." A number of its top technical talent said the internet company was betraying its idealistic principles, even as its business-minded officials worried that the protests would damage its chances to secure more business from the Defense Department.

About 4,000 Google employees signed a petition demanding "a clear policy stating that neither Google nor its contractors will ever build warfare technology." A handful of employees also resigned in protest, while some were openly advocating the company to cancel the Maven contract.

Months before it became public, senior Google officials were worried about how the Maven contract would be perceived inside and outside the company, The New York Times reported this week. By courting business with the Pentagon, they risked angering a number of the company's highly regarded A.I. researchers, who had vowed that their work would not become militarized.

Jim Mattis, the defense secretary, had reached out to tech companies and sought their support and cooperation as the Pentagon makes artificial intelligence a centerpiece of its weapons strategy. The decision made by Google on Friday is a setback to that outreach.

But if Google drops out of some or all of the competition to sell the software that will guide future weaponry, the Pentagon is likely to find plenty of other companies happy to take the lucrative business. A Defense Department spokeswoman did not reply to a request for comment on Friday.

Ms. Greene's comments were reported earlier by Gizmodo.

The money for Google in the Project Maven contract was never large by the standards of a company with revenue of $110 billion last year — $9 million, one official told employees, or a possible $15 million over 18 months, according to an internal email.

But some company officials saw it as an opening to much greater revenue down the road. In an email last September, a Google official in Washington told colleagues she expected Maven to grow into a $250 million-a-year project, and eventually it could have helped open the door to contracts worth far more; notably a multiyear, multibillion-dollar cloud computing project called JEDI, or Joint Enterprise Defense Infrastructure.

Whether Google's Maven decision is a short-term reaction to employee protests and adverse news coverage or reflects a more sweeping strategy not to pursue military work is unclear. The question of whether a particular contract contributes to warfare does not always have a simple answer.

When the Maven work came under fire inside Google, company officials asserted that it was not "offensive" in nature. But Maven is using the company's artificial intelligence software to improve the sorting and analysis of imagery from drones, and some drones rely on such analysis to identify human targets for lethal missile shots.

Google management had told employees that it would produce a set of principles to guide its choices in the use of artificial intelligence for defense and intelligence contracting. At Friday's meeting, Ms. Greene said the company was expected to announce those guidelines next week.

Google has already said that the new artificial intelligence principles under development precluded the use of A.I. in weaponry. But it was unclear how such a prohibition would be applied in practice and whether it would affect Google's pursuit of the JEDI contract.

Defense Department officials are themselves wrestling with the complexity of their move into cloud computing and artificial intelligence. Critics have questioned the proposal to give the entire JEDI contract, which could extend for 10 years, to a single vendor. This week, officials announced they were slowing the contracting process down.

Dana White, the Pentagon spokeswoman, said this week that the JEDI contract had drawn "incredible interest" and more than 1,000 responses to a draft request for proposals. But she said officials wanted to take their time.

"So, we are working on it, but it's important that we don't rush toward failure," Ms. White said. "This is different for us. We have a lot more players in it. This is something different from some of our other acquisition programs because we do have a great deal of commercial interest."

Ms. Greene said the company probably would not have sought the Maven work if company officials had anticipated the criticism, according to notes on Ms. Greene's remarks taken by a Google employee and shared with The Times.

Another person who watched the meeting added that Ms. Greene said Maven had been "terrible for Google" and that the decision to pursue the contract was done when Google was more aggressively going after military work.

Google does other, more innocuous business with the Pentagon, including military advertising on Google properties and Google's ad platform, as well as providing web apps like email.

Meredith Whittaker, a Google A.I. researcher who was openly critical of the Maven work, wrote on Twitter that she was "incredibly happy about this decision, and have a deep respect for the many people who worked and risked to make it happen. Google should not be in the business of war."

Even though the internal protest has carried on for months, there was no indication that employee criticism of the deal was dying down.

Earlier this week, one Google engineer — on the company's internal message boards — proposed the idea of employees protesting Google Cloud's conference at the Moscone Center in San Francisco in July with a campaign called "Occupy Moscone Center," fashioned after the Occupy Wall Street protests.

That engineer resigned from the company this week in protest of Maven and planned for Friday to be his last day. But he said he was told on Friday morning to leave immediately, according to an email viewed by The Times.

Peter W. Singer, who studies war and technology at New America, a Washington research group, said many of the tools the Pentagon was seeking were "neither inherently military nor inherently civilian." He added, "This is not cannons and ballistic missiles." The same software that speeds through video shot with armed drones can be used to study customers in fast-food restaurants or movements on a factory floor.

Mr. Singer also said he thought Google employees who denounced Maven were somewhat naïve, because Google's search engine and the video platform of its YouTube division have been used for years by warriors of many countries, as well as Al Qaeda and the Islamic State.

"They may want to act like they're not in the business of war, but the business of war long ago came to them," said Mr. Singer, author of a book examining such issues called "LikeWar," scheduled for publication in the fall.

DAISUKE WAKABAYASHI reported from San Francisco and **SCOTT SHANE** reported from Baltimore. **CADE METZ** contributed reporting in San Francisco.

CHAPTER 6

Assessing the Effects and Future of Drone Warfare

The United States has been using drone warfare for nearly two decades, and assessing its casualties, appropriate time and place of use, collateral damage and whether it truly curtails terrorist activity is crucial to refining foreign and military policy for the future. Unintended loss of civilian life continues. Pakistan's Taliban named a new leader, Mufti Noor Wali Mehsud, following a United States drone strike that killed the previous leader. C.I.A. drone operations in the Sahara have expanded. Furthermore, other countries, such as Russia, have been developing their own drones, among other military technologies.

The Wounds of the Drone Warrior

BY EYAL PRESS | JUNE 13, 2018

IN THE SPRING OF 2006, Christopher Aaron started working 12-hour shifts in a windowless room at the Counterterrorism Airborne Analysis Center in Langley, Va. He sat before a wall of flat-screen monitors that beamed live, classified video feeds from drones hovering in distant war zones. On some days, Aaron discovered, little of interest appeared on the screens, either because a blanket of clouds obscured visibility or because what was visible — goats grazing on an Afghan hillside, for instance — was mundane, even serene. Other times, what unspooled before Aaron's eyes was jarringly intimate: coffins being carried through the streets after drone strikes; a man squatting in a field to defecate after a meal (the excrement generated a heat signature that glowed on infrared); an imam speaking to a group of 15 young boys in the courtyard of his madrasa. If a Hellfire missile killed the target, it occurred to Aaron as he stared at the screen, everything the imam might have told his pupils about America's war with their faith would be confirmed.

The infrared sensors and high-resolution cameras affixed to drones made it possible to pick up such details from an office in Virginia. But as Aaron learned, identifying who was in the crosshairs of a potential drone strike wasn't always straightforward. The feed on the monitors could be grainy and pixelated, making it easy to mistake a civilian trudging down a road with a walking stick for an insurgent carrying a weapon. The figures on-screen often looked less like people than like faceless gray blobs. How certain could Aaron be of who they were? "On good days, when a host of environmental, human and technological factors came together, we had a strong sense that who we were looking at was the person we were looking for," Aaron said. "On bad days, we were literally guessing."

Initially, the good days outnumbered the bad ones for Aaron. He wasn't bothered by the long shifts, the high-pressure decisions or the strangeness of being able to stalk — and potentially kill — targets from thousands of miles away. Although Aaron and his peers spent more time doing surveillance and reconnaissance than coordinating strikes, sometimes they would relay information to a commander about what they saw on-screen, and "60 seconds later, depending on what we would report, you would either see a missile fired or not," he said. Other times, they would trail targets for months. The first few times he saw a Predator drone unleash its lethal payload — the camera zooming in, the laser locking on, a plume of smoke rising above the scorched terrain where the missile struck — he found it surreal, he told me. But he also found it awe-inspiring. Often, he experienced a surge of adrenaline, as analysts in the room exchanged high-fives.

Aaron's path to the drone program was unusual. He grew up in Lexington, Mass., in a home where red meat and violent video games were banned. His parents were former hippies who marched against the Vietnam War in the 1960s. But Aaron revered his grandfather, a quiet, unflappable man who served in World War II. Aaron also had a taste for exploration and tests of fortitude: hiking and wandering through the woods in Maine, where his family vacationed every summer, and wrestling, a sport whose demand for martial discipline captivated him. Aaron attended the College of William & Mary in Virginia, where he majored in history, with a minor in business. A gifted athlete with an air of independence and adventurousness, he cut a charismatic figure on campus. One summer, he traveled to Alaska alone to work as a deckhand on a fishing boat.

During Aaron's junior year, in 2001, he woke up one morning to a phone call from his father, who told him that the twin towers and the Pentagon had been attacked. Aaron thought instantly of his grandfather, who served for three years as a military police officer on the European front after the attack on Pearl Harbor. He wanted to do something similarly heroic. A year later, after spotting a pamphlet at the William & Mary career-services office for the National Geospatial-Intelligence Agency, a national-security agency that specializes in geographical and imagery analysis, he applied for a job there.

Aaron began working as an imagery analyst at the N.G.A. in 2005, studying satellite pictures of countries that had no link to the war on terror. Not long after he arrived, an email circulated about a Department of Defense task force that was being created to determine how drones could help defeat Al Qaeda. Aaron answered the call for volunteers and was soon working at the Counterterrorism Airborne Analysis Center. He found it exhilarating to participate directly in a war he saw as his generation's defining challenge. His pride deepened as it became clear that the task force was having a significant impact and that the use of drones was increasing.

Aaron spent a little over a year at the task force, including several months in Afghanistan, where he served as the point of contact between the drone center in Langley and Special Forces on the ground. After this, he worked for a private military contractor for a while. In 2010, an offer came from another contractor involved in the drone program to serve as an imagery-and-intelligence analyst. But as Aaron mulled the terms, something strange happened: He began to fall apart physically. The distress began with headaches, night chills, joint pain. Soon, more debilitating symptoms emerged — waves of nausea, eruptions of skin welts, chronic digestive problems. Aaron had always prided himself on his physical fitness, but suddenly he felt frail. Working for the contractor was out of the question. "I could not sign the paperwork," he said. Every time he sat down to try, "my hands stopped working — I was feverish, sick, nauseous."

Aaron went back to Lexington to live with his parents and try to recuperate. He was 29 and in the throes of a breakdown. "I was very, very unwell," he told me. He consulted several doctors, none of whom could specify a diagnosis. In desperation, he experimented with fasting, yoga, Chinese herbal medicine. Eventually, his health improved, but his mood continued to spiral. Aaron couldn't muster any motivation. He spent his days in a fog of gloom. At night, he dreamed that he could see — up close, in real time — innocent people being maimed and killed, their bodies dismembered, their faces contorted in agony. In one recurring dream, he was forced to sit in a chair and watch the violence. If he tried to avert his gaze, his head would be jerked back into place, so that he had to continue looking. "It was as though my brain was telling me: Here are the details that you missed out on," he said. "Now watch them when you're dreaming."

It has been almost 16 years since a missile fired from a drone struck a Toyota Land Cruiser in northwest Yemen, killing all six of its passengers and inaugurating a new era in American warfare. Today, targeted killings by drones have become the centerpiece of U.S. counterterrorism policy. Although the drone program is swathed in secrecy — the C.I.A.

and the military share responsibility for it — American drones have been used to carry out airstrikes in at least eight different countries, analysts believe. Over the past decade, they have also provided reconnaissance for foreign military forces in half a dozen other countries. According to the Bureau of Investigative Journalism, a London-based organization that has been tracking drone killings since 2010, U.S. drone strikes have killed between 7,584 and 10,918 people, including 751 to 1,555 civilians, in Pakistan, Afghanistan, Yemen and Somalia. The U.S. government's figures are far lower. It claims that between 64 and 116 noncombatants outside areas of active hostilities were killed by drones between 2009 and 2016. But as a report published last year by the Columbia Law School Human Rights Clinic and the Sana'a Center for Strategic Studies noted, the government has failed to release basic information about civilian casualties or to explain in detail why its data veers so significantly from that of independent monitors and NGOs. In Pakistan, Somalia and Yemen, the report found, the government officially acknowledged just 20 percent of more than 700 reported strikes since 2002.

"Kill chain" operations expanded under Barack Obama, who authorized roughly 500 drone strikes outside active conflict zones during his presidency, 10 times the number under George W. Bush. (This number does not include strikes carried out in Iraq, Afghanistan and Syria.) These operations have continued to grow under President Trump, who oversaw five times as many lethal strikes during his first seven months in office as Obama did during his last six months, analysts believe. According to the Bureau of Investigative Journalism, last year U.S. airstrikes more than tripled in Yemen and Somalia, where the Trump administration circumvented restrictions on operations outside war zones that were put in place in 2013. The administration has also made these operations even less transparent than under Obama, who received widespread criticism on this score.

The escalation of the drone wars has been met with strikingly little congressional or popular opposition. Unlike the policy of capturing and interrogating terrorism suspects that was adopted after Sept. 11, which fueled vigorous debate about torture and indefinite detention, drone warfare has been largely absent from public discourse. Among ordinary citizens, drones seem to have had a narcotizing effect, deadening the impulse to reflect on the harm they cause. Then again, the public rarely sees or hears about this harm. The sanitized language that public officials have used to describe drone strikes ("pinpoint," "surgical") has played into the perception that drones have turned warfare into a costless and bloodless exercise. Instead of risking more casualties, drones have fostered the alluring prospect that terrorism can be eliminated with the push of a button, a function performed by "joystick warriors" engaged in an activity as carefree and impersonal as a video game. Critics of the drone program have sometimes reinforced this impression. Philip Alston, the former United Nations special rapporteur on extrajudicial executions, warned in 2010 that remotely piloted aircraft could create a "PlayStation mentality to killing" that shears war of its moral gravity.

But the more we have learned about the experiences of actual drone fighters, the more this idea has been revealed as a fantasy. In one recent survey, Wayne Chappelle and Lillian Prince, researchers for the School of Aerospace Medicine at Wright-Patterson Air Force Base in Fairborn, Ohio, drew on interviews that they and other colleagues conducted with 141 intelligence analysts and officers involved in remote combat operations to assess their emotional reactions to killing. Far from exhibiting a sense of carefree detachment, three-fourths reported feeling grief, remorse and sadness. Many experienced these "negative, disruptive emotions" for a month or more. According to another recent study conducted by the Air Force, drone analysts in the "kill chain" are exposed to more graphic violence — seeing "destroyed homes and villages," witnessing "dead bodies or human remains" — than most Special Forces on the ground.

Because the drone program is kept hidden from view, the American public rarely hears about the psychic and emotional impact of seeing such footage on a regular basis, day after day, shift after shift. Compared with soldiers who have endured blasts from roadside bombs — a cause of brain injuries and PTSD among veterans of the wars in Iraq and Afghanistan — the wounds of drone pilots may seem inconsequential. But in recent years, a growing number of researchers have argued that the focus on brain injuries has obscured other kinds of combat trauma that may be harder to detect but can be no less crippling. Drone warfare hasn't eliminated these hidden wounds. If anything, it has made them more acute and pervasive among a generation of virtual warriors whose ostensibly diminished stress is belied by the high rate of burnout in the drone program.

As the volume of drone strikes has increased, so, too, have the military's efforts to attend to the mental well-being of drone warriors. Last year, I visited Creech Air Force Base in Nevada to interview drone pilots about their work. Forty minutes north of Las Vegas, Creech is a constellation of windswept airstrips surrounded by sagebrush and cactus groves. It is home to some 900 drone pilots who fly missions with MQ-9 Reapers in numerous theaters. Creech also has a group of embedded physiologists, chaplains and psychologists called the Human Performance Team, all of whom possess the security clearances required to enter the spaces where drone pilots do their work, in part so that they can get a glimpse of what the pilots and sensor operators experience.

A psychologist on the team named Richard (who, like most of the airmen I spoke to, asked to be identified by only his first name) told me that, two weeks into the job, he poked his head into a ground control station just as the crew was "spinning up for a strike." A veteran of the Marine Corps, he felt a surge of adrenaline as he watched the screen flash. Then he put the incident out of mind. A few weeks later, he was at his son's band concert, and as the national anthem played and he peered up at the Stars and Stripes, the memory came back. "I'm looking up at the flag, but I could see a dead body," he said. He was shaken, but he couldn't say anything to his family because the operation was classified.

Drone warriors shuttle back and forth across such boundaries every day. When their shifts end, the airmen and women drive to their subdivisions alone, like clerks in an office park. One minute they are at war;

the next they are at church or picking up their kids from school. A retired pilot, Jeff Bright, who served at Creech for five years, described the bewildering nature of the transition. "I'd literally just walked out on dropping bombs on the enemy, and 20 minutes later I'd get a text — can you pick up some milk on your way home?" Bright enjoyed serving in the drone program and believed that he was making a difference, a sentiment I heard repeatedly at Creech. But other airmen in his unit struggled to cope with stress, he said — there were divorces and some cases of suicide.

Unlike office-park employees, drone operators cannot reveal much about how their day went because of classification restrictions. Unlike conventional soldiers, they aren't bolstered by the group solidarity forged in combat zones. Richard told me that when he was in the Marines, "there was a lot of camaraderie, esprit de corps." Although service members at Creech can get close to their co-workers, at the end of every shift they go home, to a society that has grown increasingly disconnected from war.

Before the drone personnel at Creech make their way home, some drop by the Airman Ministry Center, a low-slung beige building equipped with a foosball table, some massage chairs and several rooms where pilots and sensor operators can talk with clergy. A chaplain named Zachary told me that what most burdened the airmen he spoke to was not PTSD; it was inner conflicts that weighed on the conscience. He mentioned one pilot he met with, who asked, "I'm just curious: What is Jesus going to say to me about all the killing I've done?" Despite their distance from the battlefield, drone operators' constant exposure to "gut-wrenching" things they watched on-screen — sometimes resulting directly from their own split-second decisions, or conversely, from their inability to act — could cause them to lose their spiritual bearings and heighten their risk of sustaining a very different kind of battle scar: what some psychologists, as well as Zachary, have described as a "moral injury."

The term is not new. It appeared in the 1994 book "Achilles in Vietnam," by the psychiatrist Jonathan Shay, who drew on Homer's epic war poem the "Iliad" to probe the nature of the wounds afflicting veterans of the Vietnam War. Shay read the "Iliad" as "the story of the undoing of Achilles' character," which, he argued, unravels when his commander, Agamemnon, betrays his sense of "what's right," triggering disillusionment and the desire "to do things that he himself regarded as bad." Experiencing such disillusionment might not seem as traumatic as coming under enemy fire or seeing a comrade die. Shay disagreed. "I shall argue what I've come to strongly believe through my work with Vietnam veterans: that moral injury is an essential part of any combat trauma," he wrote. "Veterans can usually recover from horror, fear and grief once they return to civilian life, so long as 'what's right' has not also been violated."

Fifteen years later, the term "moral injury" began to appear more frequently in the literature on the psychic wounds of war, but with a slightly different meaning. Where Shay emphasized the betrayal of what's right by authority figures, a new group of researchers expanded the focus to include the anguish that resulted from "perpetrating, failing to prevent or bearing witness to acts that transgress deeply held moral beliefs," as a 2009 article in the journal Clinical Psychology Review proposed. In other words, they defined it as a wound sustained when soldiers wading through the fog of war betrayed themselves, through harmful acts they perpetrated or watched unfold. This definition took shape against the backdrop of the wars in Iraq and Afghanistan, chaotic conflicts in which it was difficult to distinguish between civilians and insurgents, and in which the rules of engagement were fluid and gray.

One author of the Clinical Psychology Review article was Shira Maguen, a researcher who began to think about the moral burdens of warfare while counseling veterans at a PTSD clinic in Boston. Like most V.A. psychologists, Maguen was trained to focus on the aftershocks of fear-based trauma — I.E.D. blasts that ripped through soldiers' Humvees, skirmishes that killed members of their unit. The link between PTSD and such "life-threat" events was firmly established. Yet in many of the cases she observed, the source of distress seemed to lie elsewhere: not in attacks by the enemy that veterans had survived, but in acts they had committed that crossed their own ethical lines. "I was hearing about experiences where people killed and they thought they were making the right decision," Maguen told me recently, "and then they found out there was a family in the car."

To find out how heavy the burden of killing actually was, Maguen, who is now a staff psychologist at the V.A. Medical Center in San Francisco, began combing through databases in which veterans of conflicts dating back to the Vietnam War were asked if they had killed someone while in uniform. In some cases, the veterans were also asked whom they killed — combatants, prisoners, civilians. Maguen wanted to see if there might be a relationship between taking another life and debilitating consequences like alcohol abuse, relationship problems, outbursts of violence, PTSD. The results were striking: Even when controlling for different experiences in combat, she found, killing was a "significant, independent predictor of multiple mental health symptoms" and of social dysfunction.

In San Francisco, Maguen convened groups where veterans came together and talked about the killing they had done. In the V.A. no less than in the military, this was a taboo subject, so much so that clinicians often refer to it euphemistically, if at all. The veterans in Maguen's groups didn't speak much about fear and hyperarousal, emotions linked to PTSD. Mostly, they expressed guilt and self-condemnation. "You feel ashamed of what you did," one said. Others described feeling unworthy of forgiveness and love. The passage of time did little to diminish these moral wounds, Maguen found. Geographic distance didn't lessen them much either. She recounted the story of a pilot who was haunted by the bombs he had dropped on victims far below. What troubled him was, in fact, precisely his distance from them — that instead of squaring off against the enemy in a fair fight, he had killed in a way that lacked valor. Obviously not all pilots felt this way. But the story underscored the significance of something Maguen has come to regard as more important than proximity or distance in shaping moral injury — namely, how veterans made sense of what they had done.

"How you conceptualize what you did and what happened makes such a big difference," she said. "It makes all the difference."

The meaning and magnitude of moral injury remains contested. "It is not widely accepted by the military or the psychological community," Wayne Chappelle, of the School of Aerospace Medicine at Wright-Patterson Air Force Base, told me, adding that he did not believe it was prevalent among drone operators. This was somewhat surprising, because Chappelle was an author of the study revealing that many drone warriors struggled with lasting negative emotions after strikes, feeling "conflicted, angry, guilty, regretful." But the idea that war may be morally injurious is a charged and threatening one to many people in the military. Tellingly, Chappelle described moral injury as "intentionally doing something that you felt was against what you thought was right," like the wanton abuse of prisoners at Abu Ghraib. The definition used by researchers like Maguen is at once more prosaic and, to the military, potentially more subversive: Moral injury is sustained by soldiers in the course of doing exactly what their commanders, and society, ask of them.

By the time I met Christopher Aaron (whose given last name was left out of this article at his request), he had spent several years recuperating from his experience in the drone program. We first talked in a pub, not far from where he was living at the time. Aaron is now 37, with thick dark hair and a muscular build. He has a calm, Zen-like bearing, honed in part through yoga and meditation, but there was a trace of worry in his eyes and a degree of circumspection in his voice, particularly when he was pressed for details about particular missions (he emphasized that he could not talk about anything classified). At the pub, we spoke for two hours and agreed to continue talking over lunch the next day, so that he could pace himself. On my way to that appointment, my cellphone rang. It was Aaron, calling to reschedule. Our meeting the previous day had triggered a flood of anxiety, aggravating the pain in his back during the night.

Some analysts immediately feel that their work has left an emotional residue. In Aaron's case, the feeling unfolded gradually, coinciding with a shift in worldview, as his gung-ho support for the "war on terror" gave way to growing doubts. The disillusionment crept up in stages, starting, he realized in retrospect, a few months after he returned from Afghanistan. Although he felt proud of the work he did to help establish the drone program, he also started to wonder when the war's objective was going to be achieved. It was around this time that his manager asked him if he wanted to obtain resident C.I.A. employment status and become a career intelligence officer, which required taking a lie-detector test used to screen employees. Aaron said yes, but halfway through the test, after losing circulation in his arms and feeling hectored by the questions, he got up and abruptly left. The next day, Aaron told his manager that he had reconsidered.

Aaron ended up taking a trip to California instead, renting a motorcycle and riding all the way up the coast to Alaska, where he spent a week at a monastery on a small island, sleeping in a wood-framed chapel surrounded by spruce trees. Aaron grew up attending an Eastern Orthodox church, and the experience was faith-reaffirming. When he went back to the East Coast, he felt refreshed. But he was also out of money, so he went back to work in a field where he could easily land a job, with a military-and-intelligence contractor.

By now, Aaron's idealism had waned. It receded further when, at the end of 2008, the contractor sent him back to Afghanistan. The first time he was there, in 2006, the war on terror seemed to be hastening the defeat of Al Qaeda and the Taliban. Now it seemed to Aaron not only that progress had stalled, but that things were sliding backward. "We were actually losing control of vast areas of the country," he said, even as the number of drone strikes was "four or five times higher" than before. The escalation under President Obama had begun.

As it happened, Aaron had taken with him to Afghanistan a copy of George Orwell's "1984." He had read the book in high school and, like most people, remembered it as a dystopian novel about a totalitarian police state. This time, what stuck in his mind was a book-within-the-book written by Emmanuel Goldstein, the rumored leader of the resistance, titled "The Theory and Practice of Oligarchical Collectivism." In the book, Goldstein describes the onset of a "continuous" war, waged by "highly trained specialists" on the "vague frontiers" of Oceania — an opaque, low-intensity conflict whose primary purpose was to siphon off resources and perpetuate itself. ("The object of waging a war is always to be in a better position in which to wage another war," Orwell writes.) Aaron had an eerie sense that a perpetual war was exactly what the "war on terror" was becoming.

As his disillusionment deepened, events that Aaron dismissed before as unavoidable in any war began to weigh more heavily on him. He recalled days when the feed was "too grainy or choppy" to make out exactly who was struck. He remembered joking with his peers that "we sometimes didn't know if we were looking at children on the ground or chickens." He also thought back to the times when he would be asked "to give an assessment of a compound where they had suspicion — there was fill-in-the-blank low-level Taliban commander in a remote region in the country. And we had seen other people come in and out of the same compound over the course of the preceding two or three days. They come and say: We're getting ready to drop a bomb on there — are there any people other than the Taliban commander in this compound? I'd just say 'no' because they don't want to hear 'I don't know.' And then two days later, when they have the funeral procession in the streets that we could observe with the Predators, you'd see as opposed to carrying one coffin through the streets they're carrying three coffins through the streets."

Aaron kept his misgivings mainly to himself, but his friends noticed a change in him, among them Chris Mooney, who picked him up at the airport when he returned from Afghanistan in 2009. He and Aaron had been friends since college, when Aaron exuded confidence and enthusiasm. "He was magnetic," Mooney said. At the airport, Mooney could scarcely recognize his friend. His affect was flat, his face a solemn mask. They went to dinner, where, at one point, a patron who overheard them talking came up to Aaron to thank him for his service. Aaron thanked him back, Mooney said, but in a muted tone. Mooney didn't press him for details, but he knew that something was seriously wrong. "It wasn't the same guy," he said.

The renewed interest in moral injury can be viewed as an effort to revisit the ethical issues that have been latent in our narratives of war all along — and to address sources of trauma that some veterans and military analysts recognized years ago, before the "war on terror" had even begun. In the influential 1995 book "On Killing," Dave Grossman, a retired Army lieutenant colonel and former professor of psychology at West Point, drew on historical studies and the personal accounts of ex-combatants to argue that the psychological costs of close-range killing were often devastating. The novels and memoirs of veterans were populated with characters haunted by such incidents. In Tim O'Brien's "The Things They Carried" (1990), for example, the narrator confesses that he can't shake the image of the Vietnamese man he killed on a footpath with a grenade — his body splayed, blood glistening on his neck. Later, the narrator indicates that he didn't actually kill the man, but he was there and watched him die, "and my presence was guilt enough." Literature could evoke the inner conflicts that played on loop in the minds of veterans tormented by their troubled consciences.

In the early 1970s, some psychiatrists listened to soldiers talk about such incidents at "rap groups" organized by Vietnam Veterans Against the War. Until this point, soldiers bearing psychic wounds tended to be dismissed by the military as cowards and malingerers. ("Your nerves, hell — you are just a goddamned coward," Gen. George S. Patton snapped at a soldier in a hospital during World War II.) The Yale psychiatrist Robert Jay Lifton, who sat in on the V.V.A.W. rap groups and wrote about the disfiguring effects of killing and participating in atrocities in his 1973 book, "Home From the War," helped to recast these veterans as sympathetic figures. Lifton argued that these former soldiers were burdened not by cowardice but by the guilt and rage they felt about their involvement in a misbegotten war. In his view, moral and political questions were inseparable from Vietnam veterans' psychic wounds, to the point that he believed activism to end the war could lessen their guilt and foster healing.

When PTSD was officially recognized in the Diagnostic and Statistical Manual of Mental Disorders, in 1980, many hoped it would lead society to reckon more honestly with the ethical chaos of war. The first definition included not only survivor's guilt but also guilt "about behavior required for survival" among the potential symptoms, language that addresses acts soldiers perpetrated that went against their own moral codes. Over time, however, the moral questions that animated reformers like Lifton were reduced to "asterisks in the clinician's handbook," notes the veteran David Morris in his book, "The Evil Hours," as military psychologists shifted attention to brain injuries caused by mortar attacks and roadside bombs. One reason for this may be that focusing on such injuries, and on harmful acts in which veterans were the victims, was more comfortable for the military. Another is that it may be more comfortable for V.A. clinicians, who weren't trained to address veterans' moral pain and who "may unknowingly provide nonverbal messages that various acts of omission or commission in war are too threatening or abhorrent to hear," noted the authors of the 2009 article on moral injury in Clinical Psychology Review. Avoiding such conversations was untenable with service members returning from Iraq and Afghanistan, who were enmeshed in messy counterinsurgency campaigns that often involved close-range killing and noncombatants. According to Brett Litz, a clinical psychologist at Boston University and an author of the 2009 article, "35 percent of the traumatic events that led soldiers to seek treatment for PTSD in a recent study were morally injurious events."

When the drone program was created, it seemed to promise to spare soldiers from the intensity (and the danger) of close-range combat. But fighting at a remove can be unsettling in other ways. In conventional wars, soldiers fire at an enemy who has the capacity to fire back at them. They kill by putting their own lives at risk. What happens when the risks are entirely one-sided? Lawrence Wilkerson, a retired Army colonel and former chief of staff to Colin Powell, fears that remote warfare erodes "the warrior ethic," which holds that combatants must assume some measure of reciprocal risk. "If you give the warrior, on one side or the other, complete immunity, and let him go on killing, he's a murderer," he said. "Because you're killing people not only that you're not necessarily sure are trying to kill you — you're killing them with absolute impunity."

Langley Air Force Base in Virginia is home to part of the 480th Intelligence, Surveillance and Reconnaissance Wing, a unit of 6,000 "deployed in place" cyberwarriors. They work on what is known as the "ops floor," a dimly lit room equipped with computers streaming footage from drones circling over numerous battlefields. Many of the enlistees arrayed around the screens are in their 20s and might pass for stock traders or Google employees were it not for their military boots and combat fatigues. But the decisions they make have far weightier consequences. According to a recent study by a team of embedded Air Force researchers who surveyed personnel at three different bases, nearly one in five I.S.R. analysts said they "felt directly responsible for the death of an enemy combatant" on more than 10 occasions. One analyst told the researchers, "Some of us have seen, read, listened to extremely graphic events hundreds and thousands of times."

"Over all, I.S.R. personnel reported pride in their mission, particularly supporting successful protection of U.S. and coalition forces," the survey found. But many also struggled with symptoms of distress — emotional numbness, difficulty relating to family and friends, trouble sleeping and "intrusive memories of mission-related events," including "images that can't be unseen."

As at Creech, steps have been taken to try to mitigate the stress: shorter shifts, softer lighting, embedded chaplains and psychologists. Counteracting this is the workload, which has escalated as drones have assumed an increasingly central role in the battle against ISIS and other foes. According to Lt. Col. Cameron Thurman, who was then the unit's surgeon general, the number of acknowledged missile strikes ordered by Central Command in the United States rose substantially between 2013 and mid-2017, even as the size of the work force has remained unchanged. "You've got the same number of airmen doing the same number of mission hours but with a 1,000-percent increase in those life-and-death decisions, so of course their job is going to get significantly more difficult," he said. "You're going to have more moral overload."

A bald man with a blunt manner, Thurman sat across from me in a windowless conference room whose walls were adorned with posters of squadrons engaged in remote combat operations. Also in the room was Alan Ogle, a psychologist who was an author of the recent survey of the 480th Wing. On the PTSD scale, Ogle said, members of the unit "didn't score high," owing to the fact that few had been exposed to roadside bombs and other so-called life-threat events. What seemed to plague them more, he told me, were some forms of "moral injury."

Two members of the I.S.R. Wing described to me how changed they were by their work. Steven, who had a boyish face and sensitive eyes, is originally from a small town in the South and joined the military straight out of high school. Four years later, he told me, he no longer reacted emotionally to news of death, even after his grandmother recently died. The constant exposure to killing had numbed him. "You're seeing more death than you are normal things in life," he said. He watched countless atrocities committed by ISIS. During one mission, he was surveilling a compound on a high-visibility day when 10 men in orange jumpsuits were marched outside, lined up and, one by one, beheaded. "I saw blood," he said. "I could see heads roll." Ultimately, though, what troubled him most was not bearing witness to vicious acts committed by enemy forces but decisions he had made that had fatal consequences. Even if the target was a terrorist, "it's still weird taking another life," he said. Distance did not lessen this feeling. "Distance brings it through a screen," he said, "but it's still happening, and it's happening because of you."

Another former drone operator told me that screens can paradoxically magnify a sense of closeness to the target. In an unpublished paper that he shared with me, he called this phenomenon "cognitive combat intimacy," a relational attachment forged through close observation of violent events in high resolution. In one passage, he described a scenario in which an operator executed a strike that killed a "terrorist facilitator" while sparing his child. Afterward, "the child walked back to the pieces of his father and began to place the pieces back into human shape," to the horror of the operator. Over time, the technology of drones has improved, which, in theory, has made executing such strikes easier, but which also makes what remote warriors see more vivid and intense. The more they watch targets go about their daily lives — getting dressed, playing with their kids — the greater their "risk of moral injury," his paper concluded.

This theory is echoed by Maguen's findings. In one study, she discovered that Vietnam veterans who killed prisoners of war had especially high rates of trauma. Maguen believes the reason is that the victims were not strangers to them. "When someone is a prisoner of war, you get to know them," she explained, "you have a relationship with them: You are watching them, you are talking to them. It may be that with drone operators, they also know their subjects fairly well: They have watched them, so there's a different kind of relationship, an intimacy."

For Christopher Aaron, the hardest thing to come to terms with was that a part of him had enjoyed wielding this awesome power — that he'd found it, on some level, exciting. In the years that followed, as his mood darkened, he withdrew, sinking into a prolonged period of shame and grief. He avoided seeing friends and had no interest in intimate relationships. He struggled with "quasi-suicidal" thoughts, he told me, and with facing the depth and gravity of his wounds, a reckoning that began in earnest only in 2013, when he made his way to the Omega Institute, in Rhinebeck, N.Y., to attend a veterans' retreat run by a former machine-gunner in Vietnam.

The weather was rainy and overcast. The discussion groups he sat in on, where veterans cried openly as they talked about their struggles, were no more uplifting. But for the first time since leaving the drone program, Aaron felt that he didn't have to hide his true feelings. Every morning, he and the other veterans would begin the day by meditating together. At lunch, they ate side by side in silence, a practice called "holding space." In the evenings, he drifted into a deep sleep, unperturbed by dreams. It was the most peaceful sleep he'd had in years.

At the Omega Institute, Aaron struck up a friendship with a Vietnam veteran from Minnesota, whom he later invited up to Maine. In the fall of 2015, at this friend's suggestion, he went to a meeting of the Boston chapter of Veterans for Peace. Soon thereafter, he began to talk about funeral processions he'd witnessed after drone strikes where more coffins appeared than he expected, first with members of the group, later at some interfaith meetings organized by peace activists. It was painful to dredge up these memories; sometimes his back would seize up. But it was a form of social engagement that he found deeply relieving.

At one interfaith meeting, Aaron mentioned that he and his colleagues used to wonder if they were playing a game of "whack-a-mole," killing one terrorist only to see another pop up in his place. He had come to see the drone program as an endless war whose short-term "successes" only sowed more hatred in the long term while siphoning resources to military contractors that profited from its perpetuation. On other occasions, Aaron spoke about the "diffusion of responsibility," the whirl of agencies and decision makers in the drone program that make it difficult to know what any single actor has done. This is precisely the way the military wants it, he suspects, enabling targeted killing operations to proceed without anyone feeling personally responsible. If anything, he felt an excess of remorse and culpability, convinced that targeted killings had very likely made things worse.

Peter Yeomans, a clinical psychologist who trained with Shira Maguen, has developed an experimental treatment for moral injury rooted in the sharing of testimonials, initially at weekly meetings where veterans come together to talk among themselves, and later at a public ceremony that the participants invite members of the community to attend. One goal of the treatment is to help veterans unburden themselves of shame, Yeomans told me. Another is to turn them into moral agents who can deliver the truth about war to their fellow citizens — and, in turn, broaden the circle of responsibility for their conduct.

In early May, I attended a ceremony in a small chapel on the third floor of the V.A. Medical Center in Philadelphia, where Yeomans now works. Seated on a stage in the chapel were a number of veterans, among them a wiry man with an unkempt brown beard who sat with his eyes closed and his hands folded in his lap. His name was Andy, and when invited to speak, he told the audience that he grew up in a violent home where he watched his older brother and baby sister endure abuse, which made him want to "protect the defenseless." After high school, he enlisted in the military and became an intelligence operative in Iraq. One night, on a mission near Samarra, a city in the "Sunni triangle," a burst of sustained gunfire erupted from the second-story window of a house, and Andy said he "called air" to deliver a strike. When the smoke cleared from the leveled home, there was no clear target inside. "I see instead the wasted bodies of 19 men, eight women, nine children," Andy said, choking back tears. "Bakers and merchants, big brothers and baby sisters.

"I relive this memory almost every day," he went on. "I confess to you this reality in the hope of redemption, that we might all wince and marvel at the true cost of war."

The room fell silent as Andy went back to his chair, sobbing. Then Chris Antal, a Unitarian Universalist minister who ran the weekly meetings with Yeomans, invited members of the audience to form a circle around the veterans who had spoken and deliver a message of reconciliation to them. Several dozen people came forward and linked arms. "We sent you into harm's way," began the message that Antal recited and that the civilians encircling the veterans repeated. "We put you into situations where atrocities were possible. We share responsibility with you: for all that you have seen; for all that you have done; for all that you have failed to do," they said. Later, members of the audience were invited to come forward again, this time to take and carry candles that the veterans had placed on silver trays when the ceremony began. Andy's tray had 36 candles on it, one for each person killed in the airstrike that he called in.

Yeomans and Antal told me over dinner afterward that they believe audience participation in the ceremony was crucial. Moral injury, they pointed out, is as much about society's avoidance and denial as it is about the ethical burdens that veterans bear. Antal added that, in his opinion, grappling with moral injury requires reckoning with how America's military campaigns have harmed not only soldiers but also Iraqis and civilians in other countries.

For Antal, broadening the scope to include these civilians is both a spiritual mission and a personal one. He bears a moral injury of his own, sustained when he was serving as an Army chaplain in Afghanistan. While there, he attended transfer ceremonies in which the coffins of fallen U.S. soldiers were loaded onto transport planes to be sent home. During one such ceremony, held at Kandahar Airfield, Antal noticed drones taking off and landing in the distance, and felt a flicker of conscience. The contrast between the dignity of the ceremony, during which the fallen soldier's name was solemnly announced as "Taps" was played, and the secrecy of the drone campaign, whose victims were anonymous, jarred him. "I felt something break," he told me. In April 2016, he resigned his commission as a military officer, explaining in a letter to President Obama that he could not support a policy of "unaccountable killing" that granted the executive branch the right to "kill anyone, anywhere on earth, at any time, for secret reasons."

The secrecy of the drone program makes it riskier for people who have served in it to share their stories. Jesselyn Radack, a lawyer for national-security whistle-blowers who has worked with Aaron, told me that several former drone operators she represents have suffered retaliation for talking about their experiences (she said one client had his house raided by the F.B.I. and was placed under criminal investigation after speaking on camera to a filmmaker). After Aaron began speaking publicly about his own past, someone hacked into his email and his cell-phone, and a stream of anonymous threats began flooding his inbox. The hostile messages, calling him "scum" and warning him to "shut his big blabbermouth," were also sent to his father, whose email was likewise hacked. The barrage of threats eventually prompted Aaron to hire a law-yer to try to identify who was behind the harassment (the attorney he is working with, Joe Meadows of Bean Kinney & Korman, specializes in internet defamation), and to contact both the F.B.I. and the police.

The experience left Aaron shaken. But in recent months, he has begun to recover. He is now gainfully employed as an analyst of gold and other precious metals, a hobby he has turned into a vocation. He has started to reach out again to friends like Chris Mooney. He lives with his dog, a German shepherd, which he likes to take on walks through the forests near his home. His physical pain has mostly gone away, thanks in part to the regimen of yoga and meditation that he maintains. He still has his share of violent dreams, he told me. But he appears to have recaptured what for many years he had lost — his sense of moral purpose and, oddly enough, clarity, which is why he feels more ready to continue speaking publicly about his experience.

Not long ago, Aaron was invited to speak at an event organized by a branch of the Mennonite Church titled "Faithful Witness in a Time of Endless War." It took place on the campus of a school in Lansdale, Pa., in a small auditorium whose stage was festooned with peace quilts. Aaron approached the lectern in a brown blazer, with a somber expression. He reached forward to adjust the mic and thanked the event's organizers for inviting him to tell his story. Before sharing it, he asked for a moment of silence, "for all of the individuals that I killed or helped to kill."

EYAL PRESS is a journalist who has spent the past year as a fellow at the New York Public Library's Dorothy and Lewis B. Cullman Center for Scholars and Writers. He is at work on a book about people whose jobs take them into morally treacherous situations.

U.S. Drone Strike Kills Leader of Pakistani Taliban, Pakistan Says

BY IHSANULLAH TIPU MEHSUD | JUNE 15, 2018

ISLAMABAD, PAKISTAN — An American drone strike killed the leader of the Pakistani Taliban in a border region of Afghanistan, Pakistani officials said on Thursday.

Pakistani intelligence officials said the group's leader, Mullah Fazlullah, and four other senior commanders were killed Wednesday in a drone strike in the Afghan province of Kunar, near the Pakistani border. The officials spoke on condition of anonymity, but Mr. Fazlullah's death was later confirmed by the Pakistani Ministry of Defense.

The spokesman for the United States military in Afghanistan, Lt. Col. Martin O'Donnell, confirmed that the military had carried out a drone strike on Wednesday in Kunar. He said the target was "a senior leader of a designated terrorist organization," but he did not offer further details or confirm that Mr. Fazlullah had been killed.

Mr. Fazlullah has been the most-wanted militant in Pakistan for years. His organization has carried out hundreds of attacks against both Pakistani security forces and civilians, including an assault on a school in Peshawar in 2014 that killed 145 people or more, including at least 132 children.

In 2012, a Pakistani Taliban gunman shot Malala Yousafzai, a teenager who had been calling for more educational opportunities for girls. Ms. Yousafzai survived and received the Nobel Peace Prize in 2014.

In March, the State Department announced a $5 million reward for information leading to the arrest or capture of Mr. Fazullah.

The American drone strike came as a long stretch of tension between the United States and Pakistan seemed to be easing.

The Trump administration had been increasing pressure on Pakistan until recently, accusing the country of doing too little to help stop the Afghan Taliban's long insurgency. But in recent months, officials say, the two countries have been cooperating more in hopes of persuading the Afghan Taliban to join peace talks.

Days before the American drone strike, Pakistan's army chief, Gen. Qamar Javed Bajwa, visited Kabul to discuss the Afghan peace process and counterterrorism cooperation.

The Pakistani Taliban have not yet confirmed Mr. Fazlullah's death, which has been incorrectly reported before.

The Pakistani Taliban movement, or Tehrik-i-Taliban Pakistan, is an umbrella organization loosely uniting up to 30 groups of Pakistani militants along the tribal areas bordering Afghanistan.

Officially founded in 2007 to attack the Pakistani government and security forces, it waged a campaign of wanton violence across the country for years.

Under increasing pressure from the military, the group began splintering in 2013. Mr. Fazlullah took the leadership of the main branch in November of that year, a week after Hakimullah Mehsud, the organization's previous leader, was killed in a drone strike in the North Waziristan region of Pakistan.

He is also known as Maulana Fazlullah; the honorific maulana refers to a Muslim man revered for his religious learning or piety.

The area where the drone attack is said to have taken place is considered a stronghold of both Pakistani and Afghan Taliban fighters. The groups are separate organizations, but they often overlap in the tribal borderlands between the two countries.

Pakistani officials have been critical of American drone strikes on Pakistani soil, arguing that they are a violation of the country's sovereignty.

MUJIB MASHAL contributed reporting from Kabul, Afghanistan.

Pakistan's Taliban Names New Leader After U.S. Drone Strike

BY ZIA UR-REHMAN AND MARIA ABI-HABIB | JUNE 24, 2018

KARACHI, PAKISTAN — Pakistan's Taliban has named as its new leader, a religious scholar known for running brutal extortion rackets and opposing polio vaccination campaigns, promoting violence against health workers across the country.

The elevation of the leader, Mufti Noor Wali Mehsud, comes after a United States drone strike in Afghanistan killed the group's previous leader, Mullah Fazlullah, this month. In a statement on Saturday, Pakistan's Taliban confirmed Mr. Fazlullah's death and said it was a "matter of pride" that its leadership had been "martyred by infidels."

The group's deputy leader, Khan Sayed, who also went by the name Khalid Sajna, was killed by an American drone strike in February.

In the statement, Muhammad Khurasani, a spokesman for the group, said its executive council had appointed Mr. Mehsud, who also goes by Abu Mansoor Asim, as its new chief. It named Mufti Hazarat, a relatively unknown militant, as his deputy.

Analysts believe that the militant group, known formally as Tehrik-i-Taliban Pakistan, cannot regain its past position of strength, as military operations against the group have weakened it and created internal divisions.

"The terror outfit has been weakened significantly because of security operations across the country, especially in the tribal region," said Muhammad Amir Rana, the director of the Pak Institute for Peace Studies, a security think tank in Islamabad.

"For its newly appointed chief, overcoming the internal differences within the group and increasing its operational capabilities will be greater challenges," he said, adding that Mr. Mehsud has never been seen as a central Taliban commander.

But the threat of violence by the group has not diminished.

In Karachi, Pakistan's largest city, the news spooked many residents, as Mr. Mehsud's name is synonymous with one of the urban center's bloodiest chapters of terrorism. The group extended its influence to Karachi in 2012, at the height of its reach in the country, having spread from its base in the sprawling, isolated border region that Pakistan shares with Afghanistan.

By 2013, Mr. Mehsud had risen up the Taliban ranks to oversee Karachi, where he waged a bloody campaign of extortion and kidnapping against Pashtun traders and affluent residents, money that funded the militants' activities across Pakistan. Pashtuns, who make up a large portion of Karachi's population of more than 16 million, have traditionally fed the ranks of the Taliban.

Mr. Mehsud commanded his extortion racket in Karachi from his base in Miram Shah, a town in North Waziristan, on the border with Afghanistan, and visited the city infrequently. The militant leader forced Pashtuns from Karachi to resolve their business disputes through Taliban courts in Miram Shah, summoning civilians to make the long journey for hearings.

For those who did not heed the calls, Mr. Mehsud ensured that the Taliban meted out vengeance in Karachi, intimidating family members or threatening their businesses.

In Karachi, Muhammad Ibrahim, an owner of a small transportation company, was one of dozens summoned to Mr. Mehsud's court in Miram Shah to resolve a dispute he had with a relative.

"During that time, our community was getting regular calls from Wali's office, threatening people that they will target them or their families if they failed to pay extortion money," Mr. Ibrahim said, using Mr. Mehsud's middle name.

After a weeklong court case, Mr. Ibrahim was ordered to pay his relative about $1,600 — a small fortune in Pakistan — with a portion of that money taken by the Taliban.

A book released by Mr. Mehsud in January, called "Mehsud Revolution," discusses the Taliban's campaign against polio immunization, which the Taliban claims was used by the C.I.A. to spy on them.

The militants frequently attack vaccination teams — leading to a brief rise of the epidemic in Pakistan — and have spread propaganda that the vaccines are part of a Western conspiracy to make Muslims impotent or stunt the growth of their children.

Mr. Mehsud also claimed in the book that the Pakistani Taliban was responsible for the 2007 assassination of former Prime Minister Benazir Bhutto.

Mr. Mehsud's predecessor, Mr. Fazlullah, was infamous for ordering the failed assassination attempt of Malala Yousafzai in 2012, a teenage activist who campaigned for greater educational opportunities for girls. Ms. Yousafzai survived, and won the Nobel Peace Prize in 2014.

In Eastern Europe, U.S. Military Girds Against Russian Might and Manipulation

BY ERIC SCHMITT | JUNE 27, 2018

ORZYSZ, POLAND — Soon after a United States Army convoy crossed Poland's border into Lithuania during a major military exercise this month, two very strange things happened.

First, four Army Stryker armored vehicles collided, sending 15 soldiers to the hospital with minor injuries. But hours later, an anti-American blog claimed a child was killed and posted a photo of the accident. Lithuanian media quickly denounced the blog post as a doctored fake, designed to turn public opinion against the Americans and their Baltic ally.

The bloggers had borrowed a page from the playbook of Russia's so-called hybrid warfare, which American officials say increasingly combines the ability to manipulate events using a mix of subterfuge, cyberattacks and information warfare with conventional military might.

The military exercise, which involved 18,000 American and allied troops, offers a window into how Army commanders are countering not just Russian troops and tanks, but also twisted truths. The exercise occurred as President Trump is sidling up to Moscow by bad-mouthing NATO, calling for Russia to be readmitted into the Group of 7 industrialized nations, and planning a summit meeting with President Vladimir V. Putin of Russia next month.

American commanders say they are tuning out Mr. Trump's comments — strengthening ties to allied armies, increasing the number of troops and spies devoted to Russia, and embracing Defense Secretary Jim Mattis's newest defense strategy that focuses more on potential threats from Russia and China and less on terrorism.

"The Russians are actively seeking to divide our alliance, and we must not allow that to happen," Dan Coats, the director of national

Troops dispersed into smaller groups to simulate how to avoid sophisticated surveillance drones that could direct rocket or missile attacks against personnel or command posts.

intelligence, warned separately in a speech in France the day after the June 7 accident in Lithuania.

Over the past year, the United States and its NATO allies completed positioning about 4,500 soldiers in the three Baltic States and Poland, and have stationed several thousand other armored troops mostly in Eastern Europe as a deterrent to Russian aggression.

In Brussels, allied defense ministers met recently in advance of a NATO summit meeting in July and approved a plan to ensure that by 2020, at least 30,000 troops, plus additional attack planes and warships, can respond to aggressions within 30 days.

These tensions are part of an expanding rivalry and military buildup, with echoes of the Cold War, between Washington and Moscow.

The doctored photo of the Army accident in Lithuania was just the latest reminder of what American officials called Russia's increasing

The road march was a proving ground for enhanced technology, such as new, small reconnaissance drones and electronic-jamming equipment to thwart Russian probes.

reliance on cyberattacks and information warfare to keep its rivals off balance.

Last year, for instance, Lithuanian prosecutors investigated a claim of rape against German soldiers who were stationed in Lithuania as part of a NATO mission to deter Russia. Ultimately, the report turned out to be false. Moscow denied being involved in any disinformation campaign aimed at discrediting troops, but the incident was widely viewed as an attempt to sow divisions among the allies.

Moscow is flexing its conventional might, too, sending military forces for its own exercises along its western border with Europe and also to Syria and eastern Ukraine. Additionally, Russia is building up its nuclear arsenal and cyberwarfare prowess in what American military officials call an attempt to prove its relevance after years of economic decline and retrenchment.

In response, the Pentagon has stepped up training rotations and

A Polish tank on the move during the exercise.

exercises on the territory of newer NATO allies in the east, including along a narrow 60-mile-wide stretch of rolling Polish farmland near the Lithuanian border northeast of here called the Suwalki Gap. The corridor is sandwiched between the heavily militarized Russian exclave of Kaliningrad and Moscow's ally Belarus, and is considered NATO's weak spot on its eastern flank.

In the unlikely event of a land war, American and allied officers say, the region is where Russia or its proxies could cut off the Baltic States from the rest of Europe. Since Russia annexed Crimea and supported separatists in eastern Ukraine, Eastern Europe has felt increasingly vulnerable.

"Putin is a bird of prey," said Piotr Lukasiewicz, a retired Polish Army colonel and former Polish ambassador to Afghanistan. "He preys on weak states."

The Polish government has offered to pay the United States up to $2 billion to build a permanent military base in the country, an offer the Trump administration is weighing cautiously. American forces are, apparently for the first time, flying unarmed Reaper surveillance drones from a Polish base in the country's northwest. Nearly 2,000 Special Operations forces from the United States and 10 other NATO nations carried out one of their biggest exercises ever — Trojan Footprint 18 — in Poland and the Baltics this month.

Elsewhere in Europe, Norway agreed two weeks ago to increase the number of American Marines training there regularly, to 700 from 330, drawing an angry protest from Moscow.

The Russian military threat has changed markedly since the Soviet Union collapsed in 1991. Mr. Putin has invested heavily in modern infantry forces, tanks and artillery. Moscow has also increased its constellation of surveillance drones that can identify targets and coordinate strikes launched from other weapons.

Russia's big war game in Belarus last year — known as Zapad 2017 — involved tens of thousands of troops and raised concerns about accidental conflicts that could be triggered by such exercises, or any incursions into Russian-speaking regions in the Baltics.

The Kremlin firmly rejects any such aims and says NATO is the security threat in Eastern Europe. Gen. Joseph F. Dunford Jr., the chairman of the Joint Chiefs of Staff, met with Gen. Valery V. Gerasimov, the chief of the Russian general staff, in Helsinki, Finland, this month, in part to discuss "the current international security situation in Europe," a spokesman for General Dunford said.

A mobile American command post here in northeastern Poland reflects the Army's new realities in Eastern Europe.

Soldiers accustomed to operating from large, secure bases in Iraq and Afghanistan now practice disguising their positions with camouflage netting. Troops disperse into smaller groups to simulate avoiding sophisticated surveillance drones that could direct rocket or missile attacks against personnel or command posts. Intelligence analysts track Twitter and other social media for information on their adversaries and local sympathizers.

Members of the Army's 82nd Airborne Division during a parachute drop.

"We have to be nimble," said Brig. Gen. Richard R. Coffman, a deputy commander of the Army's First Infantry Division who is overseeing much of the American training from a command post in Orzysz.

Asked about the Russian threat, General Coffman, a third-generation Army officer from Fort Knox, Ky., echoed a sentiment of many officers interviewed over the course of three days: "To say I wasn't worried would be foolish, but it doesn't keep me up at night."

The largest American component in the $21 million exercise, called Saber Strike, consisted of roughly 3,000 soldiers from the Second Cavalry Regiment, a storied Army unit that tracks its lineage to 1836. To practice its ability to move quickly in a crisis and sustain itself along the way, the regiment drove 950 vehicles about 840 miles from its base in Vilseck, Germany, to a training range in southern Lithuania — roughly the distance from New York to Atlanta.

The road march was a proving ground for enhanced technology, such as new, small reconnaissance drones and electronic-jamming equipment to thwart Russian probes. For Lithuanian officers, many of whom have served alongside Americans in Afghanistan and Iraq, the expanded allied presence is welcome payback for the Baltic contributions to those counterterrorism campaigns of the past decade.

When it comes to Russian aggression, the Lithuanians have long memories. Hanging in the spacious office of Maj. Gen. Vitalijus Vaiksnoras, Lithuania's second-ranking officer, is a huge painting of the Battle of Orsha — from 1514 — when a force of 30,000 Lithuanians and Poles defeated 80,000 Russians.

"We cannot afford to be weak," said General Vaiksnoras, who studied in San Antonio and at Fort Leavenworth, Kan. "The Russians will take advantage of that."

Lithuania's army has grown to 10,000 full-time soldiers, a roughly 25 percent increase in the past two years, the general said. Conscription has been reinstated. And the military has bought new infantry fighting vehicles, air defenses and howitzers.

At a training range about 15 miles from the border with Belarus, Col. Mindaugas Steponavicius, commander of the Lithuanian Army's 3,000-soldier Iron Wolf brigade, said he was sharpening his forces by training with NATO partners like the United States and Germany.

He is putting aside Mr. Trump's comments and relying on soldier-to-soldier bonds to deter Russia.

"If you are a small nation, you have to have good, strong allies," said Colonel Steponavicius, who has served combat tours in Afghanistan and Iraq. "When we have such a neighbor, allies matter."

ERIC SCHMITT reported from Orzysz and Suwalki, Poland, and Vilnius, Lithuania.

2 Killed in Gaza, 4 Wounded in Israel, in Most Intense Fighting Since 2014 War

BY DAVID M. HALBFINGER | JULY 14, 2018

JERUSALEM — Two Palestinians were killed in an Israeli airstrike and four Israelis were wounded by mortar fire from Gaza on Saturday as fighting in and around the Gaza Strip escalated to what the Israeli prime minister called the most intense level since the 2014 war.

Hamas and allied Islamic militant groups fired nearly 100 projectiles at Israeli territory throughout the day, most of them mortar rounds, though rockets were fired at the city of Ashkelon.

Israel's Iron Dome air-defense batteries intercepted more than 20 of those that had the potential to do damage, the military said, but some got through. A mortar struck the courtyard of a Sderot synagogue, according to the Israeli military, and local news media reported that a house in Sderot was also hit, wounding four members of a family.

"All the house was smoke and glass," said one member, Aharon Buchris, from his hospital bed in Ashkelon, where he was treated for head and leg wounds. His wife and two daughters were also hurt. "There was a lot of blood. The television exploded, the aquarium exploded."

Azzat Magirov, 45, a neighbor, told Ynet that she had accompanied the family's two daughters, ages 14 and 15, to the hospital. She described hearing "a boom" and then shouting from the neighbors' home, before running over and finding them all bleeding. The rocket had exploded outside their living room window, and an aquarium inside the house had shattered.

"Dead fish, glass and blood covered the floor," she said. "The mother was in the kitchen and was in shock."

She added, "I hugged the children and then I was covered in blood."

Another Sderot resident, Refael Yifrah, told Kan Radio that she heard a terrifying blast around 6:15 p.m., about 15 seconds after receiving a text alert of incoming fire, but that parked cars bore the brunt of the shrapnel.

"It's better to be in Gaza where they get warning that they're going to be fired upon in one neighborhood or another and they evacuate," Ms. Yifrah said. "Here, there's an alert, no one knows where it's going to land."

The alerts kept coming all day long, and Israeli aircraft pounded at scores of what it called strictly military targets, including tunnels as well as storage sites for helium used to inflate incendiary balloons. The balloons, along with flaming kites, have scorched thousands of acres of Israeli farmland in recent months.

But Israel's targets on Saturday also included one in downtown Gaza City that Israel said was used by Hamas as a training center for urban warfare and was built atop a tunnel complex used to train fighters in underground combat.

Two Palestinian teenagers were killed and 14 people wounded in the attack, which heavily damaged the building.

Witnesses said the teenagers were relaxing near the roof of the five-story structure, little more than a concrete skeleton, when Israeli drones struck with warning shots — an Israeli practice known as "roof knocking" — before the bombing began in earnest. In video images released by the Israeli military, a large number of people can be seen running for safety on the building's rooftop after one of the initial drone strikes.

The building, in Al Katiba Square, sits within a block of Al Azhar University, various Hamas government offices and a grassy square that is a popular picnic spot for Gaza families. A mosque next door appeared largely unscathed aside from some broken windows.

Muhammad Abdelaal, 30, a guard at the ministry of religious affairs, said he raced to the top of the training center after the initial drone strikes and helped carry the two teenagers, who suffered head injuries, down to ambulances, then returned to his post to lock up.

Just then, he said, another rocket hit close to him, and he was riddled with shrapnel. He was interviewed at Shifa Hospital while soaked with blood and being treated for his wounds.

Israel said it warned Palestinians in Arabic to steer clear of Hamas locations and centers of militant activity. The initial drone strikes came more than an hour before the building was blown up, said Lt. Col. Jonathan Conricus, a spokesman for the Israel Defense Forces.

"Any uninvolved civilian casualties is regrettable, but the I.D.F. took extreme safety measures in order to signal our intentions and to warn anyone who was near what our intentions were," he said.

Saturday's fighting did not arise out of the blue: It came as a ratcheting-up of hostilities a day earlier, when an Israeli army officer was wounded by an explosive hurled across the barrier fence from Gaza, and an unarmed 14-year-old Palestinian boy was shot and killed as he climbed the fence.

The sheer number of mortars and rockets fired from Gaza was itself an escalation. Of roughly 100 launched before 8 p.m., most landed in open areas, said Brig. Gen. Tzvika Haimovic of Israel's air-defense forces. "We engaged more than 20, each one of them a huge threat," he said. "A few of them we didn't intercept, and we saw the damage." As effective as Iron Dome is, he added, no missile shield is impregnable: "There is no magic solution."

By Saturday night, the two sides were still exchanging blows, but Hamas said at about 10 p.m. that regional mediation had brought about a cease-fire. It was not immediately clear, however, that this would hold. Each side has tended to insist on getting in the last word.

And Prime Minister Benjamin Netanyahu of Israel posted a message on Twitter assuring his citizens that Israel had "struck Hamas the harshest blow since Protective Edge" — the name for Israel's 2014 military operation in Gaza — "but we shall increase the force of our attacks as necessary."

IYAD ABUHEWEILA and IBRAHIM EL-MUGHRABY contributed reporting from Gaza City.

C.I.A. Drone Mission, Curtailed by Obama, Is Expanded in Africa Under Trump

BY JOE PENNEY, ERIC SCHMITT, RUKMINI CALLIMACHI AND CHRISTOPH KOETTL | SEPT. 9, 2018

DIRKOU, NIGER — The C.I.A. is poised to conduct secret drone strikes against Qaeda and Islamic State insurgents from a newly expanded air base deep in the Sahara, making aggressive use of powers that were scaled back during the Obama administration and restored by President Trump.

Late in his presidency, Barack Obama sought to put the military in charge of drone attacks after a backlash arose over a series of highly visible strikes, some of which killed civilians. The move was intended, in part, to bring greater transparency to attacks that the United States often refused to acknowledge its role in.

But now the C.I.A. is broadening its drone operations, moving aircraft to northeastern Niger to hunt Islamist militants in southern Libya. The expansion adds to the agency's limited covert missions in eastern Afghanistan for strikes in Pakistan, and in southern Saudi Arabia for attacks in Yemen.

Nigerien and American officials said the C.I.A. had been flying drones on surveillance missions for several months from a corner of a small commercial airport in Dirkou. Satellite imagery shows that the airport has grown significantly since February to include a new taxiway, walls and security posts.

One American official said the drones had not yet been used in lethal missions, but would almost certainly be in the near future, given the growing threat in southern Libya. The official spoke on the condition of anonymity to discuss the secretive operations.

A C.I.A. spokesman, Timothy Barrett, declined to comment. A Defense Department spokeswoman, Maj. Sheryll Klinkel, said the military had maintained a base at the Dirkou airfield for several months but did not fly drone missions from there.

The drones take off from Dirkou at night — typically between 10 p.m. and 4 a.m. — buzzing in the clear, starlit desert sky. A New York Times reporter saw the gray aircraft — about the size of Predator drones, which are 27 feet long — flying at least three times over six days in early August. Unlike small passenger planes that land occasionally at the airport, the drones have no blinking lights signaling their presence.

"All I know is they're American," Niger's interior minister, Mohamed Bazoum, said in an interview. He offered few other details about the drones.

Dirkou's mayor, Boubakar Jerome, said the drones had helped improve the town's security. "It's always good. If people see things like that, they'll be scared," Mr. Jerome said.

Mr. Obama had curtailed the C.I.A.'s lethal role by limiting its drone flights, notably in Yemen. Some strikes in Pakistan and elsewhere that accidentally killed civilians, stirring outrage among foreign diplomats and military officials, were shielded because of the C.I.A.'s secrecy.

As part of the shift, the Pentagon was given the unambiguous lead for such operations. The move sought, in part, to end an often awkward charade in which the United States would not concede its responsibility for strikes that were abundantly covered by news organizations and tallied by watchdog groups. However, the C.I.A. program was not fully shut down worldwide, as the agency and its supporters in Congress balked.

The drone policy was changed last year, after Mike Pompeo, the C.I.A. director at the time, made a forceful case to President Trump that the agency's broader counterterrorism efforts were being needlessly constrained. The Dirkou base was already up and running by the time Mr. Pompeo stepped down as head of the C.I.A. in April to become Mr. Trump's secretary of state.

The Pentagon's Africa Command has carried out five drone strikes against Qaeda and Islamic State militants in Libya this year, including one two weeks ago. The military launches its MQ-9 Reaper drones from bases in Sicily and in Niamey, Niger's capital, 800 miles southwest of Dirkou.

But the C.I.A. base is hundreds of miles closer to southwestern Libya, a notorious haven for Al Qaeda and other extremist groups that also operate in the Sahel region of Niger, Chad, Mali and Algeria. It is also closer to southern Libya than a new $110 million drone base in Agadez, Niger, 350 miles west of Dirkou, where the Pentagon plans to operate armed Reaper drone missions by early next year.

Another American official said the C.I.A. began setting up the base in January to improve surveillance of the region, partly in response to an ambush last fall in another part of Niger that killed four American troops. The Dirkou airfield was labeled a United States Air Force base as a cover, said the official, who spoke on the condition of anonymity to discuss confidential operational matters.

The C.I.A. operation in Dirkou is burdened by few, if any, of the political sensitivities that the United States military confronts at its locations, said one former American official involved with the project.

Even so, security analysts said, it is not clear why the United States needs both military and C.I.A. drone operations in the same general vicinity to combat insurgents in Libya. France also flies Reaper drones from Niamey, but only on unarmed reconnaissance missions.

"I would be surprised that the C.I.A. would open its own base," said Bill Roggio, editor of the Foundation for Defense of Democracies' Long War Journal, which tracks military strikes against militant groups.

Despite American denials, a Nigerien security official said he had concluded that the C.I.A. launched an armed drone from the Dirkou base to strike a target in Ubari, in southern Libya, on July 25. The Nigerien security official spoke on the condition of anonymity to discuss the classified program.

A spokesman for the Africa Command, Maj. Karl Wiest, said the military did not carry out the Ubari strike.

Ubari is in the same region where the American military in March launched its first-ever drone attack against Qaeda militants in southern Libya. It is at the intersection of the powerful criminal and jihadist currents that have washed across Libya in recent years. Roughly equidistant from Libya's borders with Niger, Chad and Algeria, the area's seminomadic residents are heavily involved in the smuggling of weapons, drugs and migrants through the lawless deserts of southern Libya.

Some of the residents have allied with Islamist militias, including Al Qaeda in the Islamic Maghreb, which operates across Algeria, Mali, Niger and Libya.

Dirkou, in northeast Niger, is an oasis town of a few thousand people in the open desert, bordered by a small mountain range. For centuries, it has been a key transit point for travelers crossing the Sahara. It helped facilitate the rise of Islam in West Africa in the 9th century, and welcomed salt caravans from the neighboring town of Bilma.

The town has a handful of narrow, sandy roads. Small trees dot the horizon. Date and neem trees line the streets, providing shelter for people escaping the oppressive midday heat. There is a small market, where goods for sale include spaghetti imported from Libya. Gasoline is also imported from Libya and is cheaper than elsewhere in the country.

The drones based in Dirkou are loud, and their humming and buzzing drowns out the bleats of goats and crows of roosters.

"It stops me from sleeping," said Ajimi Koddo, 45, a former migrant smuggler. "They need to go. They go in our village, and it annoys us too much."

Satellite imagery shows that construction started in February on a new compound at the Dirkou airstrip. Since then, the facility has been extended to include a larger paved taxiway and a clamshell tent connected to the airstrip — all features that are consistent with the deployment of small aircraft, possibly drones.

Five defensive positions were set up around the airport, and there appear to be new security gates and checkpoints both to the compound and the broader airport.

It's not the first time that Washington has eyed with interest Dirkou's tiny base. In the late 1980s, the United States spent $3.2 million renovating the airstrip in an effort to bolster Niger's government against Col. Muammar el-Qaddafi, then the leader of Libya.

Compared with other parts of Africa, the C.I.A.'s presence in the continent's northwest is relatively light, according to a former State Department official who served in the region. In this part of Niger, the C.I.A. is also providing training and sharing intelligence, according to a Nigerien military intelligence document reviewed by The Times.

The Nigerien security official said about a dozen American Green Berets were stationed earlier this year in Dirkou — in a base separate from the C.I.A.'s — to train a special counterterrorism battalion of local forces. Those trainers left about three months ago, the official said.

It is unlikely that they will return anytime soon. The Pentagon is considering withdrawing nearly all American commandos from Niger in the wake of the deadly October ambush that killed four United States soldiers.

JOE PENNEY reported from Dirkou, Niger, ERIC SCHMITT from Washington and RUKMINI CALLIMACHI and CHRISTOPH KOETTL from New York. OMAR HAMA SALEY contributed reporting from Agadez, Niger, DIONNE SEARCEY from Dakar, Senegal, and HELENE COOPER from Washington.

Will There Be a Ban on Killer Robots?

BY ADAM SATARIANO | OCT. 19, 2018

LONDON — An autonomous missile under development by the Pentagon uses software to choose between targets. An artificially intelligent drone from the British military identifies firing points on its own. Russia showcases tanks that don't need soldiers inside for combat.

A.I. technology has for years led military leaders to ponder a future of warfare that needs little human involvement. But as capabilities have advanced, the idea of autonomous weapons reaching the battlefield is becoming less hypothetical.

The possibility of software and algorithms making life-or-death decisions has added new urgency to efforts by a group called the Campaign To Stop Killer Robots that has pulled together arms control advocates, humans rights groups and technologists to urge the United Nations to craft a global treaty that bans weapons without people at the controls. Like cyberspace, where there aren't clear rules of engagement for online attacks, no red lines have been defined over the use of automated weaponry.

Without a nonproliferation agreement, some diplomats fear the world will plunge into an algorithm-driven arms race.

In a speech at the start of the United Nations General Assembly in New York on Sept. 25, Secretary General António Guterres listed the technology as a global risk alongside climate change and growing income inequality.

"Let's call it as it is: The prospect of machines with the discretion and power to take human life is morally repugnant," Mr. Guterres said.

Two weeks earlier, Federica Mogherini, the European Union's high representative for foreign affairs and security policy, said the weapons "impact our collective security," and that decisions of life and death must remain in human hands.

Twenty-six countries have called for an explicit ban that requires some form of human control in the use of force. But the prospects for an A.I. weapons ban are low. Several influential countries including the United States are unwilling to place limits while the technology is still in development.

Diplomats have been unable to reach a consensus about how a global policy can be implemented or enforced. Some have called for a voluntary agreement, others want rules that are legally binding.

A meeting of more than 70 countries organized by the United Nations in Geneva in August made little headway, as the United States and others said a better understanding of the technology was needed before sweeping restrictions can be made. Another round of talks are expected to be held later this year.

Some have raised concerns that a ban will affect civilian research. Much of the most cutting-edge work in artificial intelligence and machine learning is from universities and companies such as Google and Facebook. But much of that technology can be adapted to military use.

"A lot of A.I. technologies are being developed outside of government and released to the public," said Jack Clark, a spokesman for OpenAI, a Silicon Valley group that advocates for more measured adoption of artificial intelligence. "These technologies have generic capabilities that can be applied in many different domains, including in weaponization."

Major technical challenges remain before any robot weaponry reaches the battlefield. Maaike Verbruggen, a researcher at the Institute for European Studies who specializes in emerging military and security technology, said communication is still limited, making it hard for humans to understand why artificially intelligent machines make decisions. Better safeguards also are needed to ensure robots act as predicted, she said.

But significant advancements will come in the next two decades, said Derrick Maple, an analyst who studies military spending for the market research firm Jane's by IHS Markit in London. As the technology changes, he said, any international agreement could be futile; countries will tear it apart in the event of war.

"You cannot dictate the rules of engagement," Mr. Maple said. "If the enemy is going to do something, then you have to do something as well. No matter what rules you put in place, in a conflict situation the rules will go out the window."

Defense contractors, identifying a new source of revenue, are eager to build the next-generation machinery. Last year, Boeing reorganized its defense business to include a division focused on drones and other unmanned weaponry. The company also bought Aurora Flight Sciences, a maker of autonomous aircrafts. Other defense contractors such as Lockheed Martin, BAE Systems and Raytheon are making similar shifts.

Mr. Maple, who has worked in the field for over four decades, estimates military spending on unmanned military vehicles such as drones and ships will top $120 billion over the next decade.

No completely autonomous weapons are known to be currently deployed on the battlefield, but militaries have been using technology to automate for years. Israel's Iron Dome air-defense system automatically detects and destroys incoming rockets. South Korea uses autonomous equipment to detect movements along the North Korean border. Mr. Maple expects more collaboration between humans and machines before there is an outright transfer of responsibility to robots. Researchers, for example, are studying how aircrafts and tanks can be backed by artificially intelligent fleets of drones.

In 2016, the Pentagon highlighted its capabilities during a test in the Mojave Desert. More than 100 drones were dropped from a fighter jet in a disorganized heap, before quickly coming together to race toward and encircle a target. From a radar video shared by the Pentagon, the drones look like a flock of migrating starlings.

There were no humans at the controls of the drones as they flew overhead, and the machines didn't look much different from those any person can buy from a consumer-electronics store. The drones were programmed to communicate with each other independently to collectively organize and reach the target.

"They are a collective organism, sharing one distributed brain for decision-making and adapting to each other like swarms in nature," William Roper, director of the Pentagon's strategic capabilities office, said at the time.

To those fearful of the advancement of autonomous weapons, the implications were clear.

"You're delegating the decision to kill to a machine," said Thomas Hajnoczi, the head of disarmament department for the Austrian government. "A machine doesn't have any measure of moral judgment or mercy."

Glossary

drone An unmanned aircraft, ship or other vehicle that is controlled remotely.

ethnic cleansing The act of mass removal or killing of people who belong to a specific ethnic or religious group within a society.

euphemism A less offensive word or expression used to indirectly convey the same meaning as an equivalent unpleasant word or expression.

jihadist A form of the Arabic word "jihad," which means struggling. It applies to the efforts of religious devotees to wage a holy war on behalf of Islam.

Predator A model of U.A.V. used by the U.S. Air Force and C.I.A. that was originally used for reconnaissance and was later augmented to carry and fire missiles.

Project Maven A Pentagon pilot program that focuses on the development of artificial intelligence to better interpret video imagery acquired from military drones.

proliferation A large increase of something; rapid production.

reconnaissance The act of observing an area in order to gather information or to locate an enemy target.

sensory isolation The deprivation of stimuli from one or more senses.

teleoperate To control a machine or device remotely.

unmanned aerial vehicle (U.A.V.) An aircraft that is controlled and flown remotely without a pilot being present in the vehicle.

Media Literacy Terms

"Media literacy" refers to the ability to access, understand, critically assess and create media. The following terms are important components of media literacy, and they will help you critically engage with the articles in this title.

angle The aspect of a news story that a journalist focuses on and develops.

attribution The method by which a source is identified or by which facts and information are assigned to the person who provided them.

balance Principle of journalism that both perspectives of an argument should be presented in a fair way.

byline Name of the writer, usually placed between the headline and the story.

commentary A type of story that is an expression of opinion on recent events by a journalist generally known as a commentator.

credibility The quality of being trustworthy and believable, said of a journalistic source.

critical review A type of story that describes an event or work of art, such as a theater performance, film, concert, book, restaurant, radio or television program, exhibition or musical piece, and offers critical assessment of its quality and reception.

editorial Article of opinion or interpretation.

fake news A fictional or made-up story presented in the style of a legitimate news story, intended to deceive readers; also commonly used to criticize legitimate news because of its perspective or unfavorable coverage of a subject.

human interest story A type of story that focuses on individuals and how events or issues affect their lives, generally offering a sense of relatability to the reader.

impartiality Principle of journalism that a story should not reflect a journalist's bias and should contain balance.

intention The motive or reason behind something, such as the publication of a news story.

interview story A type of story in which the facts are gathered primarily by interviewing another person or persons.

news story An article or style of expository writing that reports news, generally in a straightforward fashion and without editorial comment.

op-ed An opinion piece that reflects a prominent individual's opinion on a topic of interest.

paraphrase The summary of an individual's words, with attribution, rather than a direct quotation of the person's exact words.

quotation The use of an individual's exact words indicated by the use of quotation marks and proper attribution.

reliability The quality of being dependable and accurate, said of a journalistic source.

source The origin of the information reported in journalism.

style A distinctive use of language in writing or speech; also a news or publishing organization's rules for consistent use of language with regard to spelling, punctuation, typography and capitalization, usually regimented by a house style guide.

tone A manner of expression in writing or speech.

Media Literacy Questions

1. What is the intention of the article "Fatal Strike in Yemen Was Based on Rules Set Out by Bush" (on page 27)? How effectively does it achieve its intended purpose?

2. Do Eric Schmitt and Jane Perlez demonstrate the journalistic principle of impartiality in their article "U.S. Unit Secretly in Pakistan Lends Ally Support" (on page 36)? If so, how did they do so? If not, what could they have included to make their article more impartial?

3. Often, as a news story develops, a journalist's attitude toward the subject may change. Compare "The Moral Case for Drones" (on page 41) and "Drone Strikes Statistics Answer Few Questions, and Raise Many" (on page 74), both by Scott Shane. Did new information discovered between the publication of these two articles change Shane's perspective?

4. The article "Let the Military Run Drone Warfare" (on page 56) is an example of an op-ed. Identify how Adam B. Schiff's attitude and tone help convey his opinion on the topic.

5. Identify the various sources cited in the article "U.S. and Pakistan Give Conflicting Accounts of Drone Strike" (on page 117). How does Salman Masood attribute information to each of these sources in his article? How effective are Masood's attributions in helping the reader identify his sources?

6. "The Wounds of the Drone Warrior" (on page 167) is an example of a human interest story. What is the purpose of a human interest story? Do you feel this article achieved that purpose?

Citations

All citations in this list are formatted according to the
Modern Language Association's (MLA) style guide.

BOOK CITATION

THE NEW YORK TIMES EDITORIAL STAFF. *Drone Warfare*. New York: New York
   Times Educational Publishing, 2020.

ONLINE ARTICLE CITATIONS

BUMILLER, ELISABETH. "A Day Job Waiting for a Kill Shot a World Away." *The
   New York Times*, 29 July 2012, https://www.nytimes.com/2012/07/30/us
   /drone-pilots-waiting-for-a-kill-shot-7000-miles-away.html.

COOPER, HELENE. "U.S. Demands Return of Drone Seized by Chinese
   Warship." *The New York Times*, 16 Dec. 2016, https://www.nytimes
   .com/2016/12/16/us/politics/us-underwater-drone-china.html.

DAO, JAMES, AND ANDREW C. REVKIN. "A Revolution in Warfare." *The New York
   Times*, 16 Apr. 2002, https://timesmachine.nytimes.com/timesmachine
   /2002/04/16/569550.html.

GENZLINGER, NEIL. " 'Drone' Documentary Examines a New Weapon." *The
   New York Times*, 17 Nov. 2015, https://www.nytimes.com/2015/11/20
   /movies/review-drone-documentary-examines-a-new-weapon.html.

HALBFINGER, DAVID M. "2 Killed in Gaza, 4 Wounded in Israel, in Most Intense
   Fighting Since 2014 War." *The New York Times*, 14 July 2018, https://www
   .nytimes.com/2018/07/14/world/middleeast/2-killed-in-gaza-4-wounded-in
   -israel-in-most-intense-fighting-since-2014-war.html.

HARRIS, GARDINER. "Trump Administration Seeks to Expand Sales of Armed
   Drones." *The New York Times*, 19 Apr. 2018, https://www.nytimes.com/2018
   /04/19/us/politics/trump-drones-sales.html.

JAFFER, JAMEEL, AND BRETT MAX KAUFMAN. "Limit the Next President's Power
   to Wage Drone Warfare." *The New York Times*, 8 Mar. 2016, https://www

.nytimes.com/2016/03/08/opinion/limit-the-next-presidents-power-to
-wage-drone-warfare.html.

JOHNSTON, DAVID, AND DAVID E. SANGER. "Fatal Strike in Yemen Was Based
on Rules Set Out by Bush." *The New York Times*, 6 Nov. 2002, https://
timesmachine.nytimes.com/timesmachine/2002/11/06/767107.html.

KAAG, JOHN, AND SARAH KREPS. "The Moral Hazard of Drones." *The New York
Times*, 22 July 2012, https://opinionator.blogs.nytimes.com/2012/07/22/the
-moral-hazard-of-drones/.

MASOOD, SALMAN. "U.S. and Pakistan Give Conflicting Accounts of Drone
Strike." *The New York Times*, 25 Jan. 2018, https://www.nytimes.com
/2018/01/25/world/asia/us-pakistan-drone.html.

MASOOD, SALMAN. "U.S. Drone Strike Kills Militants in Pakistan but Angers
Its Government." *The New York Times*, 24 Jan. 2018, https://www.nytimes
.com/2018/01/24/world/asia/pakistan-us-drone-haqqani-network.html.

MEHSUD, IHSANULLAH TIPU. "U.S. Drone Strike Kills Leader of Pakistani
Taliban, Pakistan Says." *The New York Times*, 15 June 2018, https://www
.nytimes.com/2018/06/15/world/asia/drone-pakistani-taliban-mullah
-fazlullah.html.

THE NEW YORK TIMES. "Preventing a Free-for-All With Drone Strikes." *The
New York Times*, 16 Mar. 2017, https://www.nytimes.com/2017/03/16
/opinion/preventing-a-free-for-all-with-drone-strikes.html.

OPPEL, RICHARD A., JR. "Strikes in Pakistan Underscore Obama's Options." *The
New York Times*, 23 Jan. 2009, https://www.nytimes.com/2009/01/24
/world/asia/24pstan.html.

PENNEY, JOE, ET AL. "C.I.A. Drone Mission, Curtailed by Obama, Is Expanded
in Africa Under Trump." *The New York Times*, 9 Sept. 2018, https://www
.nytimes.com/2018/09/09/world/africa/cia-drones-africa-military.html.

PERLEZ, JANE. "Muted U.S. Response to China's Seizure of Drone Worries
Asian Allies." *The New York Times*, 18 Dec. 2016, https://www.nytimes.com
/2016/12/18/world/asia/muted-us-response-to-chinas-seizure-of-drone
-worries-asian-allies.html.

PERLEZ, JANE, AND MATTHEW ROSENBERG. "China Agrees to Return Seized Drone,
Ending Standoff, Pentagon Says." *The New York Times*, 17 Dec. 2016, https://
www.nytimes.com/2016/12/17/world/asia/china-us-drone.html.

POLLACK, KENNETH M. "Learning From Israel's Political Assassination Program." *The New York Times*, 7 Mar. 2018, https://www.nytimes.com
/2018/03/07/books/review/ronen-bergman-rise-and-kill-first.html.

PRESS, EYAL. "The Wounds of the Drone Warrior." *The New York Times*, 13 June 2018, https://www.nytimes.com/2018/06/13/magazine/veterans -ptsd-drone-warrior-wounds.html.

REHMAN, ZIA, AND MARIA ABI-HABIB. "Pakistan's Taliban Names New Leader After U.S. Drone Strike." *The New York Times*, 24 June 2018, https:// www.nytimes.com/2018/06/24/world/asia/pakistan-taliban-leader.html.

RETICA, AARON. "Drone-pilot Burnout." *The New York Times*, 12 Dec. 2008, https:// www.nytimes.com/2008/12/14/magazine/14Ideas-Section2-B-t-001.html.

SATARIANO, ADAM. "Will There Be a Ban on Killer Robots?" *The New York Times*, 19 Oct. 2018, https://www.nytimes.com/2018/10/19/technology /artificial-intelligence-weapons.html.

SAVAGE, CHARLIE. "U.S. Releases Rules for Airstrike Killings of Terror Suspects." *The New York Times*, 6 Aug. 2016, https://www.nytimes.com /2016/08/07/us/politics/us-releases-rules-for-airstrike-killings-of-terror -suspects.html.

SAVAGE, CHARLIE. "U.S. Removes Libya From List of Zones With Looser Rules for Drone Strikes." *The New York Times*, 20 Jan. 2017, https://www.nytimes .com/2017/01/20/us/politics/libya-drone-airstrikes-rules-civilian-casualties .html.

SAVAGE, CHARLIE, AND ERIC SCHMITT. "Trump Poised to Drop Some Limits on Drone Strikes and Commando Raids." *The New York Times*, 21 Sept. 2017, https://www.nytimes.com/2017/09/21/us/politics/trump-drone-strikes -commando-raids-rules.html.

SCHIFF, ADAM B. "Let the Military Run Drone Warfare." *The New York Times*, 12 Mar. 2014, https://www.nytimes.com/2014/03/13/opinion/let-the -military-run-drone-warfare.html.

SCHMIDT, MICHAEL S. "Pentagon Will Extend Military Honors to Drone Operators Far From Battles." *The New York Times*, 6 Jan. 2016, https:// www.nytimes.com/2016/01/07/us/pentagon-will-extend-military -honors-to-drone-operators-far-from-battles.html.

SCHMITT, ERIC. "American Drone Strike in Libya Kills Top Qaeda Recruiter." *The New York Times*, 28 Mar. 2018, https://www.nytimes.com/2018/03/28 /world/africa/us-drone-strike-libya-qaeda.html.

SCHMITT, ERIC. "In Eastern Europe, U.S. Military Girds Against Russian Might and Manipulation." *The New York Times*, 27 June 2018, https:// www.nytimes.com/2018/06/27/us/politics/american-allies-russia-baltics -poland-hybrid-warfare.html.

SCHMITT, ERIC. "A Shadowy War's Newest Front: A Drone Base Rising From Saharan Dust." *The New York Times*, 22 Apr. 2018, https://www.nytimes.com/2018/04/22/us/politics/drone-base-niger.html.

SCHMITT, ERIC. "Under Trump, U.S. Launched 8 Airstrikes Against ISIS in Libya. It Disclosed 4." *The New York Times*, 8 Mar. 2018, https://www.nytimes.com/2018/03/08/world/africa/us-airstrikes-isis-libya.html.

SCHMITT, ERIC. "U.S. Would Use Drones to Attack Iraqi Targets." *The New York Times*, 6 Nov. 2002, https://timesmachine.nytimes.com/timesmachine/2002/11/06/766429.html.

SCHMITT, ERIC, AND JANE PERLEZ. "U.S. Unit Secretly in Pakistan Lends Ally Support." *The New York Times*, 22 Feb. 2009, https://www.nytimes.com/2009/02/23/world/asia/23terror.html.

SHACHTMAN, NOAH. "A War of Robots, All Chattering on the Western Front." *The New York Times*, 11 July 2002, https://timesmachine.nytimes.com/timesmachine/2002/07/11/935930.html.

SHANE, SCOTT. "Drone Strikes Reveal Uncomfortable Truth: U.S. Is Often Unsure About Who Will Die." *The New York Times*, 23 Apr. 2015, https://www.nytimes.com/2015/04/24/world/asia/drone-strikes-reveal-uncomfortable-truth-us-is-often-unsure-about-who-will-die.html.

SHANE, SCOTT. "Drone Strikes Statistics Answer Few Questions, and Raise Many." *The New York Times*, 3 July 2016, https://www.nytimes.com/2016/07/04/world/middleeast/drone-strike-statistics-answer-few-questions-and-raise-many.html.

SHANE, SCOTT. "The Moral Case for Drones." *The New York Times*, 14 July 2012, https://www.nytimes.com/2012/07/15/sunday-review/the-moral-case-for-drones.html.

SHANE, SCOTT. "New Rules Set on Armed Drone Experts." *The New York Times*, 17 Feb. 2015, https://www.nytimes.com/2015/02/18/world/new-rules-set-on-armed-drone-exports.html.

SHANE, SCOTT, AND DAISUKE WAKABAYASHI. " 'The Business of War': Google Employees Protest Work for the Pentagon." *The New York Times*, 4 Apr. 2018, https://www.nytimes.com/2018/04/04/technology/google-letter-ceo-pentagon-project.html.

SHANE, SCOTT, ET AL. "How a Pentagon Contract Became an Identity Crisis for Google." *The New York Times*, 30 May 2018, https://www.nytimes.com/2018/05/30/technology/google-project-maven-pentagon.html.

SHANKER, THOM. "New Incentives for Pilots of Remote Plane." *The New York Times*, 17 Oct. 2002, https://timesmachine.nytimes.com/timesmachine/2002/10/17/429180.html.

SHATZ, ADAM. "Obama Hoped to Transform the World. It Transformed Him." *The New York Times*, 12 Jan. 2017, https://www.nytimes.com/2017/01/12/opinion/obama-hoped-to-transform-the-world-it-transformed-him.html.

WAKABAYASHI, DAISUKE, AND SCOTT SHANE. "Google Will Not Renew Pentagon Contract That Upset Employees." *The New York Times*, 1 June 2018, https://www.nytimes.com/2018/06/01/technology/google-pentagon-project-maven.html.

WALSH, DECLAN, AND ERIC SCHMITT. "U.S. Strikes Qaeda Target in Southern Libya, Expanding Shadow War There." *The New York Times*, 25 Mar. 2018, https://www.nytimes.com/2018/03/25/world/middleeast/us-bombs-qaeda-libya.html.

Index

This book is current up until the time of printing. For the most up-to-date reporting, visit www.nytimes.com.